# Praise for "A Simple Guide to I[nheritance Tax]"

"At last a book that explains all we need to know about Inheritance Tax in language that people like us can understand. We knew we needed to do something to protect our inheritance, and this book takes away the mystique and jargon and has let us take the all-important first step."

*Sally and Mark Baylis (retired midwife & PR Consultant)*


"If you are, like me, lucky enough to be a parent, you really need to read this book. Paul is very good at protecting his clients' wealth and that is why I have gone to him to put the plan together to help me protect my wealth.

As Inheritance Tax is a voluntary tax, be like me. I asked Paul to sort out my Inheritance Tax problems and estate planning. It's because he has helped me so much that I am writing such a glowing testimonial.

Thank you, Paul, for writing this book and for your help. Your experience is invaluable!"

*Philip Masters (Investment Adviser)*


"Really useful book!"

*Michael Jenner (Data Manager)*

"I found reading this book really informative and useful. I've recommended it to friends to read."

*Pamela Jenner (retired)*

"A brilliant book! Very happy to recommend. A must read – very informative, easy to understand and useful examples."

*Cheryl Pearce (Entrepreneur)*

"Read it! Act upon it! And benefit from it!"

*Dr Elizabeth Foley (Medical Consultant & Researcher)*

"If you have children and own your own home YOU NEED TO READ THIS BOOK. It's the most readable and helpful book on Inheritance Tax planning that I have come across – better still, contact the author asap."

*Mark Ainsworth (Pension Adviser)*

"Why has no-one written this book before? Thank you Paul for writing a guide in such a clear and concise way, using plain, understandable language that highlights how important Inheritance Planning is for all of us."

*Paul Veal (retired Entrepreneur)*

"This is such a thorough and informative book on an extremely challenging subject. Everybody should read it."

*Dr Robert Baylis (Consultant Anaesthetist)*


"No wonder this book has nothing but five star reviews! Written in plain English for the layman like me. Easy to understand with simple examples. I now know more about how to save inheritance tax than I thought possible. If you own your own home and have children, I thoroughly recommend this book to you."

*Steve Mills (Marketing Consultant)*


"When we read this we understood every word and it all made sense – and we didn't forget any of it"

*Peter & Sue Marchant (Domestic & Industrial Cleaning Company Owners)*

# How to Get the Best Out of This Book

Various Chancellors of the Exchequer, e.g. Nigel Lawson, George Osborne, Roy Jenkins, have described Inheritance Tax as a "voluntary tax". You only have to pay this tax if you choose to do so or do not plan properly.

The wealthiest families in the UK have long realised this. Most have taken the decision either not to pay Inheritance Tax or to reduce the amount they pay to a tiny percentage of the value of their estate.

In this book you will discover

- what Inheritance Tax is
- how Inheritance Tax works
- the actions you can take to reduce the amount of Inheritance Tax your family pay or even to avoid paying it altogether.

Section 1 outlines the various threats, including Inheritance Tax, which can prevent your family from receiving and benefitting from what you wish to pass on to them when you pass away.

Section 2 provides an overview of Inheritance Tax and how it works.

Section 3 details legitimate strategies people successfully use to control their Inheritance Tax, reducing or eliminating it altogether.

*"A Simple Guide to Inheritance Tax"* is, as it says, a *simple* guide. It is designed to give you an overview and better understanding of how this tax works, so that you can get the best out of your advisers. It is not a technical manual, even though it contains a lot of technical information. It is certainly not designed to be used as a "DIY" manual for Inheritance Tax planning. As is the case in many other fields, you can find yourself in hot water very quickly, incurring costs and problems, if you treat Inheritance Tax planning as something suitable for a "DIY" approach.

You can use this book to gain an understanding of how Inheritance Tax works, get a broad brush idea of the likely extent of your own family's likely Inheritance Tax liability, and gain an appreciation of some of the ways you may be able to control it. But it is absolutely essential that you take good professional advice when addressing your Inheritance Tax issues.

**WARNING:**

This book is a *simple guide* and cannot be taken as providing tax, investment, accountancy or any other professional advice. It is absolutely essential that you take good professional advice when addressing Inheritance Tax issues.

The authors believe this book to be accurate at the time it is written, but this is a constantly evolving field with changes in statute, case law and Revenue practice. Also there are many interactions of different taxes etc, and this book only gives an overview with a particular emphasis on the effects of Inheritance Tax in isolation from other taxes. When considering the implementation of any specific strategies it is important to take advice on the overall impact including any other tax matters which may arise.

The authors of this book, and Wills Trusts Tax Solutions LLP, make no warranties with respect to the accuracy or completeness of the book. We can accept no liability for any loss or risk which may arise directly or indirectly from reliance by yourself or by any other party on information contained in the book.

# Contents

How to Get the Best Out of This Book ............................................................................................... 5

## Section 1 - Threats ............................................................................................................. 11

Chapter 1: First Things First ............................................................................................................ 13
Chapter 2: Not Having a Will ........................................................................................................... 15
Chapter 3: Inadequate Will ............................................................................................................... 21
Chapter 4: Care Fees ......................................................................................................................... 25
Chapter 5: Divorce ............................................................................................................................ 29
Chapter 6: Creditors & Bankruptcy .................................................................................................. 31
Chapter 7: Frivolous Spending ......................................................................................................... 33
Chapter 8: Marriage after Death ....................................................................................................... 35
Chapter 9: Probate ............................................................................................................................. 37
Chapter 10: Executorship .................................................................................................................. 41
Chapter 11: Challenges to the Will ................................................................................................... 45
Chapter 12: Incapacity ...................................................................................................................... 49
Chapter 13: Inheritance Tax .............................................................................................................. 51

## Section 2 – Foundations ................................................................................................... 53

Chapter 14: What is Inheritance Tax? ............................................................................................... 55
Chapter 15: The History of Inheritance Tax ..................................................................................... 57
Chapter 16: How Inheritance Tax Works ......................................................................................... 59
Chapter 17: Nil Rate Band ................................................................................................................ 61
Chapter 18: Basic Inheritance Tax Calculations ............................................................................... 63
Chapter 19: Generational Inheritance Tax ........................................................................................ 69
Chapter 20: Lifetime Transfers ......................................................................................................... 73
Chapter 21: Exempt Transfers .......................................................................................................... 75
Chapter 22: Potentially Exempt Transfers (PETs) ........................................................................... 77
Chapter 23: Chargeable Lifetime Transfers ...................................................................................... 85
Chapter 24: Gifts with Reservation of Benefit ................................................................................. 91
Chapter 25: Pre-owned Assets Tax ................................................................................................... 95
Chapter 26: Administration of Inheritance Tax .............................................................................. 101

## Section 3 - Strategies ....................................................................................................... 107

Chapter 27: Strategies for Reducing Inheritance Tax ..................................................................... 109
Chapter 28: Reduce the Inheritance Tax Value of Your House ..................................................... 111
Chapter 29: Inheritance Tax Pre-Payment Trust ............................................................................ 115
Chapter 30: Reclaim Inheritance Tax You Paid on an Inheritance ................................................ 119
Chapter 31: Change the Tax on an Inheritance You have already Received .................................. 121
Chapter 32: Family Gift Trusts ....................................................................................................... 123
Chapter 33: Gift & Loan Trusts ...................................................................................................... 127
Chapter 34: Discounted Gift Trusts ................................................................................................ 131
Chapter 35: Invest in Agricultural Land ......................................................................................... 135
Chapter 36: Invest in Buildings of Outstanding Interest ................................................................ 137
Chapter 37: Invest in Land of Outstanding Beauty or of Historic or Scientific Interest ................ 145

| | |
|---|---|
| Chapter 38: Invest in Woodland | 153 |
| Chapter 39: Invest in Qualifying Works of Art | 157 |
| Chapter 40: Invest in Your Own Trading Business | 167 |
| Chapter 41: Invest in Unquoted Shares | 171 |
| Chapter 42: Invest in EIS Shares or Portfolios | 173 |
| Chapter 43: Create Your Own Family Investment Company | 179 |
| Chapter 44: Have Assets Redirected before You Even Receive Them | 181 |
| Chapter 45: Turn Your House into an Inheritance Tax Reduction Strategy | 185 |
| Chapter 46: Obtain a Controlling Interest in a Public Company | 189 |
| Chapter 47: Spend More | 191 |
| Chapter 48: Emigrate to a Country with Low Inheritance Tax | 193 |
| Chapter 49: Emigrate to a High Inheritance Tax Threshold Country | 195 |
| Chapter 50: Emigrate to a No Inheritance Tax Country | 197 |
| Chapter 51: Gift Assets and Survive 7 Years | 201 |
| Chapter 52: Exempt Gifts | 203 |
| Chapter 53: Gifts up to £3,000 per Annum | 205 |
| Chapter 54: Gifts for Family Maintenance | 207 |
| Chapter 55: Small Gifts | 209 |
| Chapter 56: Gifts for Weddings and Civil Ceremonies | 211 |
| Chapter 57: Regular Gifts from Income | 213 |
| Chapter 58: Gifts for National Purposes | 217 |
| Chapter 59: Gifts to Political Parties | 219 |
| Chapter 60: Gifts to Charities | 221 |
| Chapter 61: Pensions | 225 |
| Chapter 62: Die in Public Service | 227 |
| Chapter 63: The Next Steps | 229 |

| | |
|---|---|
| **Appendix** | **231** |
| Trusts | 233 |
| About the Authors | 239 |

## Section 1 - Threats

Section 1 outlines the various threats, including Inheritance Tax, which can prevent your family from receiving and benefitting from what you wish to pass on to them when you pass away.

## Chapter 1:  First Things First

The first step in Inheritance Tax planning is getting your estate in order.

Most of our clients want their estate to pay less Inheritance Tax because they want their family to benefit from more of their wealth. That is why, as estate planners, we always advise our clients to deal with "first things first", so that those they wish to benefit from that wealth are the ones who will actually benefit.

This means addressing the various threats which can seriously deplete the wealth you will be leaving them.

It is considered good estate planning practice to address all the threats rather than just focussing on Inheritance Tax planning. It is dangerous to ignore the other threats to the legacy you wish to leave to your children. In fact it is important to address most or all of those threats first before you even begin to focus on Inheritance Tax. Unless you do this you may find you are not actually choosing the best solutions and have to re-visit your decisions when you look at those other threats.

These are the 12 major threats to a family's inheritance which we have outlined in the next 12 chapters.

## Chapter 2: Not Having a Will

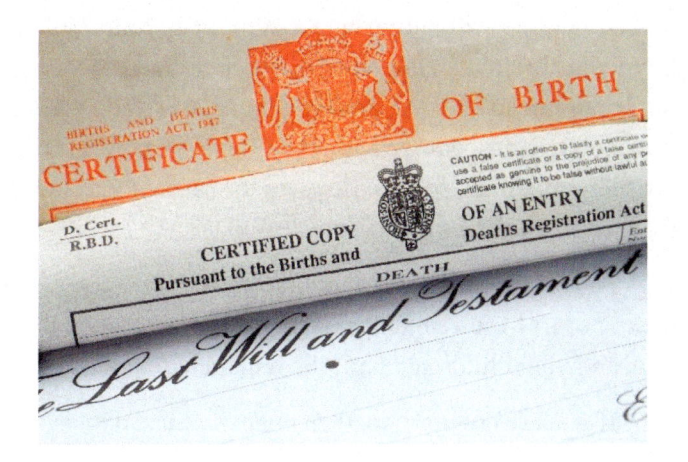

We all have a Birth Certificate, many of us have a Marriage Certificate, and we will all inevitably at some point have a Death Certificate. My question is, "where is the valid Will to go alongside the Death Certificate?"

Many people do not even want to think about making a Will, perhaps unconsciously believing that if they do not do anything to prepare for death this means death will never come for them.

There is no legal requirement to have a Will but if you don't the government will decide where your assets are distributed when you die, not you. That is not usually where you would have chosen. It could even all go to the state! What is also clear is that any Inheritance Tax liability will be higher if you do not have a Will.

# Rules of Intestacy

If you die without leaving a Will, or if your Will is not legally valid for any reason, your estate is divided according to the "rules of intestacy". An amazing number of Wills we check for people are not legally valid, even though many have been prepared by solicitors, so in those cases the rules of intestacy will apply even though they had written a Will.

If you are married, the first £270,000 goes to your spouse. 50% of the remainder of the estate also goes to your spouse, and your children inherit the remainder equally.

If you are not married, then none of your estate passes to a co-habiting partner.

## Example 1 - Intestate Unmarried Couple

Adam Clark and Marion Lewis lived together for many years. They viewed themselves as a married couple who had simply never got around to the formalities of a marriage ceremony and obtaining a legal certificate of marriage. They also never got around to writing Wills.

Adam bought the house in which he and Marion lived before he met Marion, and it was therefore just registered in his name.

When Adam died, Marion assumed she would inherit their home. When someone dies without a valid Will their estate follows the rules of intestacy. In this case, their children inherited the house along with all Adam's other assets. Marion inherited nothing, as the rules of intestacy do not recognise any rights of inheritance between co-habiting couples.

Marion had a legal right to challenge the distribution of the house to the children as she had lived in the house with Adam for over two years, but this action would be costly and there was no guarantee she would win it. Instead she just accepted the situation, living in a house which could no longer be regarded as even partially belonging to her. She remained reliant on the goodwill of the children to allow her to continue living there and no longer had the financial security she and Adam had always assumed would automatically be hers.

This problem could easily have been avoided if Adam had written a Will which stated his house would pass to Marion on his death, or at least that she had the right to live in it until her own death.

If, as you read this, you recognise this as being similar to your situation, or if it simply reminds you that you are not comfortable with your situation, please contact us urgently. Trying to help clients who have lost a large part of their estate at the time as losing their partner is one of the most harrowing parts of our profession, and is something that could easily be avoided if they consulted with us before it happened.

## Example 2 - Intestate Married Couple, Loss of Home

Malcolm & Barbara Hobbs never bothered to write Wills as they were legally married and therefore believed that they would each inherit the other's estate on death.

They have the following assets:

| | |
|---|---|
| Home | £640,000 |
| Investments | £20,000 |
| Cash | £10,000 |
| Furniture & Sundry Possessions | £30,000 |
| **Total Estate** | **£700,000** |

They each own half of the assets (including their home, which is owned as "Tenants in Common"[1] and therefore 50% each). They therefore each have an estate of £350,000.

When Malcolm dies, as he has not written a Will the first £310,000 of his £350,000 estate goes to Barbara. This is less than his £320,000 share of their home. Even if Barbara gives her children all the investments and cash she received from Malcolm there is still a shortfall. The reality is that she needs all of this anyway in order to maintain her standard of living.

---

[1] A couple may own their house together either as "Joint Tenants" or as "Tenants in Common". Joint Tenants both own the whole property together rather than each owning their own share. This means when one of the Joint Tenants dies, the remaining Joint Tenant automatically owns the whole property. Tenants in Common each own their own share of the property, which is usually 50% each. This means when one of the Tenants in Common dies, he or she can decide who will own that share of the property, just as is the case with any other personally owned assets.

So Barbara is forced to sell the marital home so that she can pass to her children the amount she is legally required to give them.

## Example 3 - Intestate Married Couple, Additional IHT

Gary and Christine Long never bothered to write Wills as they were legally married and therefore believed that they would each inherit the other's estate on death.

They have the following assets:

| | |
|---|---:|
| Home | £750,000 |
| Property Portfolio | £2,100,000 |
| Investments | £850,000 |
| Cash | £250,000 |
| Furniture & Sundry Possessions | £50,000 |
| **Total Estate** | **£4,000,000** |

They each own half of the assets (including their home, which is owned as "tenants in common" and therefore 50% each). They therefore each have an estate of £2,000,000.

When Gary dies, as he has not written a Will the first £1,135,000 of his estate goes to Christine.

The remaining £865,000 is for their children, but first there is £146,000 Inheritance Tax to pay, as shown in the following calculation:

| | |
|---|---|
| **Total Taxable Estate** | **£865,000** |
| Gary's Nil Rate Band | £325,000 |
| Gary's Residence Nil Rate Band | £175,000 |
| Total Allowances | £500,000 |
| **Taxable Estate** | **£365,000** |
| Inheritance Tax @ 40% | £146,000 |

You will find a full explanation of these calculations later in the book, but what it is important to note at this point is that there is a £146,000 Inheritance Tax bill to pay at this point, whereas no Inheritance Tax would have been due if everything had passed to Christine or, even better, into trusts with her as a beneficiary.

At best this means Gary and Christine's family have paid £146,000 Inheritance Tax before this would have been necessary if Gary had written a Will passing most or all of his estate to Christine. But if Gary and Christine had written appropriate Wills using some of the techniques outlined in this book they need not have paid any of that Inheritance Tax at all. So at worst this is a total and unnecessary loss of £146,000.

## Chapter 3: Inadequate Will

Even if you do have a Will, unless it is very carefully drafted it could result in your assets being distributed to very different people from those you intended to enjoy them. 95% of the Wills we have examined do not protect the assets in any way at all. They do not ensure the benefits are really received by the people the person intended.

The first step in a proper estate plan is to have a Will that is correctly drafted to protect your assets from the other major threats and ensure they are passed on to those you wish to benefit.

Asking a solicitor to draft your Will does not necessarily guarantee that what you want to happen is what will actually happen. A solicitor will usually simply act on your instructions, and is not obliged to point out that the end result might not be what you had intended.

## Example 4 - Bad Will - Wife Loses Income

Philip and Alison Walsh live a comfortable married life with a nice home, an investment property portfolio, some cash and other investments. This is **all** owned by Philip, as follows:

| | |
|---|---|
| Home | £500,000 |
| Property Portfolio | £2,500,000 |
| Investments | £50,000 |
| Cash | £50,000 |
| Furniture & Sundry Possessions | £50,000 |
| **Total Estate** | **£3,150,000** |

Somebody told Philip that he will save Inheritance Tax if he passes everything except the family home to their children, so he wrote his Will to do this.

When Philip died the Inheritance Tax calculation was:

| | |
|---|---|
| **Total Taxable Estate** | **£2,650,000** |
| Philip's Nil Rate Band | £325,000 |
| Total Allowances | £325,000 |
| **Taxable Estate** | **£2,325,000** |
| Inheritance Tax @ 40% | £930,000 |

On his death, Alison lost all her income in retirement, which she was getting (through Philip) from the rental income on the property, as this now belonged to the children.

As you can see, there was certainly an Inheritance Tax bill on his death. This had to be paid by selling some of the properties in the property investment portfolio, as there was not enough to cover it in the cash and other investments left by Philip.

## Example 5 - Couple lose their home and retirement income

This is a true case, not an example made up to illustrate a point. I have therefore not used any names or figures so it is not possible to identify the couple.

We met a successful man who had built up a good business that allowed him to buy a nice home and four investment properties. This man instructed his solicitor to draft "Mirror Wills", i.e. Wills for himself and his wife that were identical. In an attempt to avoid Inheritance Tax he had the Wills state that half the home and half the investment property portfolio were to pass to their children rather than to the surviving spouse.

The couple planned to use the investment property portfolio to provide them with an income in retirement.

The way the Wills were written meant that when the first of the couple died, the remaining spouse would only own half the home and half the investment required to provide them with an income. They would therefore lose half their planned retirement income. They could also be thrown out of their home, or at least forced to share it with some or all of their children or anyone their children decided should live there.

This otherwise intelligent business man could not believe that a solicitor would have produced a document for him that could result in such a catastrophic disaster. He therefore refused to believe that this could be the result of the way his and his wife's Wills were written. But it was. The solicitor had not done anything wrong, as he had acted on his client's instructions and written the Will exactly how the client wanted it written. But he did not feel it was his responsibility to point out the major disadvantages of writing it this way.

As you can see, it is very important not only to write a Will but also to write that Will properly so that it achieves what you really want to achieve and in the best and most tax efficient way.

## Chapter 4: Care Fees

Funding Long Term Care Fees is a bigger financial threat to most estates than Inheritance Tax. While Inheritance Tax can never take more than 40% of an estate, Long Term Care Fees can consume 100%. It is standard practice for local authorities to take and sell the family home to cover the cost of Care Fees. It is estimated that 70,000 homes are sold every year to fund long term care.

Long Term Care is not regarded as "medical care", so you have to pay for this personally rather than receiving it through the NHS.

A quick bit of internet research shows that, in our area, nursing home fees are at least £56,000 a year. In a recent BUPA survey one person spent over 20 years in a care home.

### Example 6 - 90 Year Old Loses His House

In one recently reported example, neighbours of a 90 year old man rang social services because they knew he was living on his own and they had not seen him out and about recently. When social services arrived they did not find any particular medical problems but arranged for him to go into care for an assessment just in case.

The initial assessment did not find any major problems either, but it nevertheless turned into a 9 months stay in a care home. During the first 12 weeks in care the Local Authority paid for this, but after that they put a charge on the man's house.

By the time the man left the care home his house had been sold to pay the cost of the care fees. He had lost his home, and had to buy a greatly downgraded home in an area where he knew nobody.

This man would not have lost his home if he had taken the right action in advance to protect it.

### Example 7 - Mother Leaves Non-existent House to Daughter

Laura Osborne had a house and a small amount of cash in the bank.

As Laura got older and more frail, her daughter, Georgina gave up her job to look after her mother. Her son, Mark, continued working and did not do anything to help his mother and sister.

Laura wanted to show her gratitude towards her daughter for her sacrifice, and so wrote a new Will giving Laura the house and Mark the small amount of cash. She felt this was very fair, given all that Laura had given up for her sake. She did not discuss this with an experienced estate planner, who would have advised her of the potentially disastrous consequences of her decision, but simply gave these instructions to her solicitor, who followed them exactly as given.

In the fullness of time, Laura developed dementia. Georgina could no longer look after her, so Laura went into a nursing home. The local authority insisted Laura's house was sold to pay for her nursing care.

When Laura passed away she no longer had a house, but the balance of the sale proceeds after care costs was in her bank account. According to the Will, Georgina would get the house (which no longer existed), and Mark would get all the cash (which was now Laura's entire estate).

So Mark got everything and Georgina got nothing. Knowing that had his mum not gone into care and had to sell her house he would have got virtually nothing, Mark felt no obligation to put things right and help his sister. He kept everything for himself.

Clearly this was a very different result from what Laura had intended.

With proper estate planning put in place before the problem arises you can substantially or completely remove the threat of Care Fees decimating your estate.

## Chapter 5: Divorce

When our children get married, we all hope that it will be "Till death do us part" and that they will have a long and happy marriage.

Unfortunately, nearly half of all marriages (42%) end in divorce.

If your children's marriages fail they can lose some, if not all, of their inheritance.

Most of us have worked hard for many years to create any wealth that we might have e.g. the family home plus, maybe, a business, investment properties, a holiday home, pension schemes, life insurances, investments and cash.

It would be a shame and totally unnecessary for any inheritance your children might receive from you to be put at risk through a failed marriage. With proper estate planning, you can protect your children's inheritance for them.

## Example 8 - Son Loses Half of His Inheritance to Divorce

Beryl Davies died, leaving her £500,000 estate to her only son, Clive, who was married to Hilary.

Clive's marriage failed and the divorce settlement gave Hilary half of Clive's assets – including half of this recent inheritance. His original £500,000 inheritance was now reduced to £250,000.

If Beryl had followed proper estate planning guidance none of the estate she left to Clive would have disappeared in a divorce settlement.

## Chapter 6: Creditors & Bankruptcy

About 600 bankruptcies and 3,800 county court judgements a day prove that, for a variety of reasons, people get into extreme financial difficulty. Often this is not their fault at all, but caused by circumstances completely beyond their control.

The top 12 reasons for Bankruptcy and pressure from creditors are:

- Using credit for living expenses
- Student debt
- Job loss
- Business failure
- Reduced income
- Divorce
- Unexpected expenses
- Bad budgeting & overspending
- Mortgage arrears
- Gambling or other addictions
- Long term sickness

- Unpaid fines or bills

With proper estate planning you can ensure Bankruptcy & pressure from Creditors doesn't mean that your beneficiaries have to lose their inheritance.

## Example 9 - Son Loses His Inheritance in a Business Venture

Keith Johnson left his son, Matthew, an estate of £400,000.

Matthew was a self-employed civil engineer. He had a long term contract with a large construction company, and employed a number of staff to service this contract. Unfortunately the construction company went into liquidation owing Matthew several months of fees. Matthew had to pay his own contractors and also had to pay for all the materials used in the contract, even though he had received nothing from his customer.

The total debt incurred was £300,000. By the time all the legal costs had been paid Matthew's entire inheritance from his father was lost.

If Keith had used the principles outlined later in this book the £400,000 he had left his son would have been protected. Matthew would have had access to this money to start over again rather than having lost everything through no fault of his own.

# Chapter 7: Frivolous Spending

Half of all people who win the lottery are broke within just a few years.

For a lot of people, inheriting a lot of money is a bit like winning the lottery.

Regrettably, for some, the old adage "Easy come - Easy go" is all too real. This doesn't make them "Bad People" it just makes them "Bad at Money Management".

Even "Financially Sensible" people can go off the rails and become "Financially Delinquent". Especially if they start mixing with the wrong people or come under the wrong influence.

"Bad Money Management" or "Financial Delinquency" and children/grandchildren squandering their inheritance is a common problem. With proper estate planning you can ensure this issue does not arise with your children and grandchildren.

## Example 10 - Sensible Daughter Loses Her Inheritance because of Boyfriend's Bad Influence

Andrew Miller left his estate of £600,000 to his daughter Julie.

When she inherited this sum, Julie found that many acquaintances became good friends. They invited her out for many meals, but expected her to pay for them!

Some of these new-found friends introduced Julie to the pleasures of non-prescription drugs. She resisted at first, but they insisted that it was now quite normal and everybody did it. They also said it would help her feel better as she mourned the loss of her father. So she tried it out and it became quite a regular habit.

In no time at all Julie found that she had spent most of her inheritance. She also found that her new friends had either disappeared or just become acquaintances again.

With careful planning Andrew could have ring-fenced and protected the inheritance he passed on to Julie so that it couldn't have been squandered. If he had done this she would still have had access to her inheritance, but would have had infinitely more security. Her "friends" couldn't have influenced her to squander the money and this tragedy would not have happened.

## Chapter 8: Marriage after Death

Not many people pass away wanting their surviving spouse to stay a widow/widower with all the loneliness that can bring. Most widowers do in fact remarry and many widows do also.

As an example, if a wife dies first and at some point her husband remarries, in the new marriage:

1      If the husband dies first the new wife may inherit everything. The children will inherit nothing.

2      If that marriage fails, the new wife could get half or more of the children's inheritance.

# Example 11 - Children Lose their Inheritance to Step-Siblings

Ralph and Pauline Wilson had three children, Jeremy, Claire and Lauren. They each wrote a Will passing their entire estate to each other, but to their children Jeremy and Claire, if the other had already passed away.

Pauline died first, leaving around £700,000 to Ralph.

After a couple of years, Ralph met Dinah. Ralph and Dinah fell in love and married.

Ralph died first, and his entire estate went to Dinah.

Dinah then met James Gray. After a couple of years Dinah and Jeremy got married. James had two children, Ashley and Naomi.

Dinah died and her estate, including the inheritance from Ralph, went to James.

James had no contact with Jeremy or Claire, and left his estate to his own children, Ashley and Naomi.

Ashley and Naomi, who Ralph and Pauline had never known, therefore inherited the entire estate Ralph and Pauline had intended to pass on to their children Jeremy and Clair – who now inherited nothing at all from their parents.

## Chapter 9: Probate

"Probate" is the legal right to deal with someone's property, money and possessions when they die. Probate is obtained by the personal representatives of the person who has died. Until Probate is obtained, nobody has any right to use or distribute any of the deceased's assets, other than to pay the Inheritance Tax and to pay for the funeral costs.

Before Probate can be obtained, the personal representatives must work out how much Inheritance Tax is due, pay this, and receive acknowledgement from HM Revenue & Customs (HMRC) that it has been paid. Only then can they apply for Probate.

Obtaining Probate is a very time consuming process. According to the government, a straightforward case should take around 16 weeks, but our experience shows it usually takes much longer. We have found that currently it is taking between 6 and 13 months even for straightforward cases. Complex cases can take a lot longer. Also, if there are any queries on the Probate application it is passed to another department and can be held up there for many more weeks before the queries are addressed. Bear in mind that these timescales are *after* the Inheritance Tax has been calculated and paid and HMRC have informed the Probate Registry of this. In the meantime, as stated, the assets of the deceased cannot be distributed and the family cannot use them.

In a newspaper article in December 2021 we read of two brothers who had been waiting 10 months for Probate and still saw no sign of it being granted. In the meantime their estate was losing £1,000 a month in interest on a loan which could not be repaid until the house was sold, which itself could not happen until Probate was granted.

In a statement in Parliament in November 2020, MP Liz Saville Roberts said *"One family I heard of ... were required [during the wait for Probate] to spend £30,000 on repairs in relation to the deceased's estate, and of course that was at a time they did not have the funds to be able to afford that. This is not an isolated case."* During the same debate another MP said *"The administration of an estate can be a stressful and difficult time for families, especially when they have just lost loved ones. Gaining access to funds quickly is important, as not all families have money readily available, and they may need the probate to gain access to those funds."*

The larger the estate the longer it takes to get Probate and to be able to distribute the legacy to the beneficiaries. The family of a person who dies and leaves a house worth £500,000 will be granted Probate (and be able to distribute the assets of the estate) much quicker than the family of someone who leaves a £1 million house, a business, a couple of investment properties, and some stocks and shares.

It is critical to have one's affairs in order to stop unnecessary delays in distributing an estate to the beneficiaries. Also, some assets should be set aside so that they do not form part of the Probate bureaucracy and can be distributed within weeks rather than months or even years.

# Chapter 10: Executorship

Probate is obtained by the personal representatives of the person who has died. These are either the "Executors", appointed in the Will, or the family members of the deceased if there is no Will. We will refer to them as Executors from now on as the same rules apply to both.

Many people appoint their children as their Executors. Being Executor can be a stressful, time-consuming and thankless job that carries substantial legal and financial responsibility which frequently makes them unpopular with the beneficiaries. This can cause family dissension where family members are the Executors. It can also cause great distress, and sometimes catastrophic financial consequences, to those family members expected to perform the task. We always advise our clients to have a professional executor.

As already stated, before Probate can be obtained, the Executors must work out how much Inheritance Tax is due, pay this, and receive acknowledgement from HM Revenue & Customs (HMRC) that it has been paid.

After they have obtained Probate, the Executors have to distribute the Estate in accordance with the wishes of the deceased (or in accordance with the Rules of Intestacy if there is not a valid Will).

It is the responsibility of the Executors to determine exactly what the assets and liabilities of the Estate are, who exactly are the beneficiaries, and exactly how much each beneficiary should receive. This is generally a complex and onerous task even in the most modest estates.

Firstly, determining the assets and liabilities of the deceased is not as simple as it might sound. Sometimes it can be very difficult to account for all the assets, and this may take a lot of work and skill. There may also be hidden creditors who do not come to light until late in the day, or even known creditors who are actually owed something very different from what the Executors initially believe. This can particularly be the case with the Inheritance Tax debt.

If it turns out that the Estate is insolvent (in other words, the liabilities are greater than the assets), the Executors are responsible for ensuring the debts are settled in the correct order, so that all the priority debts are paid before non-priority debts, and that any remaining debtors are paid the right percentages of their debts.

The Executors have to work out exactly what taxes have to be paid, not just the Inheritance Tax, but also Income Tax and Capital Gains Tax. The latter taxes will probably continue to increase while the Executors are doing their work, as it is not just the tax liabilities of the deceased that are concerned here, but also the taxes that arise from income and gains in the estate after the death.

Determining who the beneficiaries are can also be more complex than it sounds. The Will may not be as clear on this as it first appears. Or it may mention a beneficiary quite clearly but the Executors have no idea who this is or how to contact them. Adding to this complication, there may be people who are not named in the Will but who believe they have a legal right to some of the Estate. Usually the wishes of the deceased as stated in the Will take priority, but there are some instances where this is not necessarily the case.

It is also the responsibility of the Executors to protect the assets of the Estate. This includes ensuring everything is properly secured, as well as fully insured.

If the Executors get any of this wrong they can be held personally liable even if they acted in good faith.

In one real case an Executor made a mistake in the estate planning calculations before distributing the estate. He thought he had paid the correct amount of Inheritance Tax, but had not. He paid HM Revenue & Customs (HMRC) £1.15 Million and then, believing he had settled the Inheritance Tax bill in full he distributed the remaining estate to the Beneficiaries.

A year later HMRC contacted him and asked him to pay the "next" £1.15 million. He realised to his horror that the Inheritance Tax bill was not £1.15 million, but £11.5 million to be paid in 10 annual instalments.

At first the Executor contacted all the Beneficiaries, explained the error, and asked them to refund some of the money he had distributed to them. They refused.

He then explained to HMRC what had happened, and told them there was no money left in the Estate and therefore he could not make the payment this year or the following 8 years.

The response from HMRC was that this was not their problem. He was the Executor and was legally responsible for paying the full remaining debt of £10.35 million plus interest over the next 8 years.

That Executor did not have the millions required, so he lost all his money and other assets and went bankrupt.

We meet people all the time who wish they had never taken on the responsibility of being an Executor for a deceased friend or relative. It is a thankless and stressful task that should be delegated to a professional and experienced Executor who can "untangle" the estate and distribute it to the correct beneficiaries quicker and more efficiently than an amateur but well-meaning friend or relative. A good Executor can work for a pre-agreed fixed fee and will often save the family far more than that fee simply from the way they handle the estate.

## Chapter 11: Challenges to the Will

Even if you deal with all the previously outlined threats there is still no guarantee that your wishes will be fulfilled unless you also take action to reduce the likelihood of successful challenges to your Will.

Someone can challenge your Will for one or more of the following reasons:

1. The Will has not been "properly executed";
2. You did not have the required "mental capacity";
3. You did not fully understand and approve the content of the Will;
4. You were "unduly influenced" when preparing the Will;
5. The Will is a forgery or is based on fraudulent information given to the person making the Will;
6. There is a later valid Will;

7. The Will does not truly reflect your wishes, due to a clerical error or failure by the person drawing it up to understand your true intentions;
8. The Will does not make adequate provision for a spouse, former spouse, child, or other person who was financially dependent on you.

In most cases it is down to the person challenging your Will to show that one of the above reasons applies. However, if the challenge is that you lacked capacity or that you did not fully understand and approve the Will it is down to the Executor to prove that this is *not* the case. If the Executor cannot prove this, the challenge will be accepted by the Court.

We always ensure there is legal evidence with the Will to make it far less likely anyone would try to challenge the Will.

## Example 12 - Witnesses Did Not See the Will Being Signed

Geoffrey Foster decided to save costs by using a "do-it-yourself" Will. He wanted to leave everything to his wife, Shirley.

After he had written and signed his Will, Geoffrey remembered there were supposed to be witnesses, so he took the Will next door and asked his neighbours to sign as witnesses.

When Geoffrey died, his adult children were annoyed that they had not been left anything and asked a solicitor to help them challenge the Will.

The first thing the solicitor did was to check the Will had been properly executed, so he contacted the witnesses and asked them to confirm they had been present when the Will was signed. The witnesses said they did not see Geoffrey sign the Will.

This was enough evidence to show that the Will had not been properly executed, and it was ruled as not valid. As there was no earlier Will, the Rules of Intestacy applied. Shirley inherited what she was entitled to under the Rules of Intestacy, and the rest passed to the children, even though this was clearly not what Geoffrey had intended.

## Example 13 - Lack of Capacity

Edith Hicks was a widow with two adult sons, Dylan and Martin, who were not financially dependent on her. Dylan spent a lot of time with Edith when she fell ill, but Martin had never once bothered to visit her. Edith decided to pass all her wealth to Dylan.

When Edith died, and Martin realised he was getting nothing, he asked his solicitor to challenge the Will. The solicitor sent a *"Larke v Nugus"* request to the person who drew up Edith's Will, asking them to detail all the circumstances in which the Will was prepared.

Edith was 79 and unfortunately in poor health when she instructed her Will-writer. Given her age and her state of health, the Will-writer should have taken appropriate actions to satisfy himself that she fully understood what she was doing, and he should have made contemporaneous notes of this and ensured those notes were held on file. He had neglected to do this. In those circumstances the Court ruled that on the balance of probabilities Edith did not have the mental capacity required in order to provide instructions for a Will.

In an earlier Will, Edith had left her estate equally to Dylan and Martin. As the Court had ruled her latest Will was not valid due to lack of capacity, her earlier Will prevailed. Martin therefore received half of Edith's estate even though this was not her wish and was not what she had stated in her final Will.

These examples show just how important it is that the person helping you prepare your Will takes all the right steps and makes sure all the necessary evidence is kept with the Will just in case there is a challenge.

# Chapter 12: Incapacity

There often comes a time when, because of the frailty that tends to come with advancing years, or owing to some form of health problem or incapacity, a person is unable to manage their financial affairs or personal welfare. If this were to happen, you would need someone to act on your behalf. This person is known as your "Attorney".

## Example 14 - Elderly Lady Loses Control of Her Life

Alice Parker has now reached the stage where it is difficult for her to manage her own affairs without help. As she has already reached that stage it is no longer legally possible for her simply to have members of her family provide that help. She has to allow the Office of the Public Guardian to appoint someone as her Attorney. This person would usually be a solicitor, charging Alice reasonably high fees, and also acting in a very cautious manner (regardless of what Alice actually wanted to do).

So Alice has now completely lost control of her own life, as well as having to pay someone she doesn't know to control it for her.

Having as your Attorney someone to manage your affairs who you know, trust and who understands you is far more preferable, and also far less costly, than having a court official appointed to do the job.

Giving a family member or trusted friend Lasting Power of Attorney in advance ensures that, if the worst happens, you can rest assured that both your financial affairs and personal welfare are in safe hands. Proper estate planning means your estate is far less likely to be substantially depleted because of the cost of managing your affairs.

Once you have already begun to lose capacity to act on your own behalf, such as in the above example of Alice, it is too late to arrange for a family member or trusted friend to help you. What we encourage our clients to do is to set up this arrangement in advance, while they are still fit and healthy, and then ensure the document is held in secure storage. It is only released from storage when evidence is provided that they no longer have capacity, or when they themselves say they now wish that friend or relative to act. That way they can rest assured everything is taken care of before any problems arise, but also that nobody can take control of their life before this is necessary.

# Chapter 13: Inheritance Tax

And now we come to the subject of this book. Inheritance Tax.

As we have outlined above, there are 12 major threats to your estate before you even get to Inheritance Tax:

- Lack of a Will
- Poorly written Will
- Care Fees
- Divorce
- Creditors
- Bankruptcy
- Frivolous spending by Beneficiaries
- Marriage after death
- Probate costs and delays
- Executorship issues
- Challenges to the Will
- Incapacity

When you consider all these different threats it is likely that something on this list will devastate the estate you wish to leave to your family unless you do something about them all.

A properly structured Will would sweep up all these threats in one go and better prepare the estate to reduce the Inheritance Tax.

Experience shows that many people leave their Inheritance Tax Planning too late. Early planners are more likely to substantially or completely remove their Inheritance Tax burden.

We have seen multi-million pound estates without any Inheritance Tax liability as a result of proper estate planning, proving that much is possible.

# Section 2 – Foundations

Section 2 provides an overview of Inheritance Tax and how it works.

# Chapter 14: What is Inheritance Tax?

Inheritance Tax is a tax charge on transfers of capital by an individual. In fact, at one time it was actually called "Capital Transfer Tax". It is most commonly charged on the value of an estate when an individual dies but, in certain circumstances, it may also be charged during an individual's lifetime.

The law regarding Inheritance Tax is mostly contained in the *Inheritance Tax Act 1984 (IHTA 1984)*, although this has to be read, considered and interpreted along with the many Finance Acts which have been issued since that date.

# Chapter 15: The History of Inheritance Tax

The origin of Inheritance Tax was the need to raise money for war.

It was first introduced in 1694, as part of the Stamps Act, to help finance the Nine Years War. In the *Stamps Act 1694* it was a fixed sum of five shillings on all estates larger than £20.

In 1780, more money was needed to finance British troops attempting to put down the American Revolution, so the fixed sum was increased to a graduated rate and a "Legacy Duty" was also introduced.

In 1881, the law requiring tax to be paid on capital passed to the next generation was strengthened. It now became impossible for the beneficiaries to receive their estate without first proving that the relevant tax had been paid. This is still the case today. Before the beneficiaries can receive their legacy they first have to pay any Inheritance Tax due.

The highest rate of Estate Duty payable on death increased substantially over time, rising from the original 8% to:

- 15% in 1907
- 20% in 1914
- 40% in 1919
- 50% in 1930
- 60% in 1939
- 65% in 1940
- 75% in 1946
- 80% in 1949
- **85% in 1969**

Estate Duty was replaced in 1975 with Capital Transfer Tax. The highest rate of Capital Transfer Tax on death was initially 75% and remained at this level until 1984, when it was reduced to 60%.

What we now know as Inheritance Tax was introduced in the *Inheritance Tax Act 1984* at a rate of 40%.

The current rate of 40% is the lowest it has been for over 100 years.

The government now has to find ways to reduce soaring national debt, which is currently around £2.5 billion. One way to do this would be to increase the rate of Inheritance Tax and/or lower the Inheritance Tax threshold. This could be politically more expedient than increasing the rates of other taxes.

# Chapter 16: How Inheritance Tax Works

Inheritance Tax, which is currently 40%, is payable on the worldwide assets of UK individuals and on the UK assets of non-UK individuals.

It is assessed on the transfer of assets, usually on the death of an individual. With certain exceptions it includes all the assets they owned at the date of death plus any assets given away up to seven years before the date of death.

It is also assessed on certain transfers made by an individual during his or her lifetime.

Inheritance Tax is assessed on transfers of an *individual*, not of a family or a couple. Whether the assets are kept within the family or passed outside the family makes no difference to whether or not Inheritance Tax is charged or to the amount of Inheritance Tax payable. There are, though, certain exceptions, perhaps the most important of which is that no tax is paid on a transfer to a spouse or civil partner.

## Chapter 17: Nil Rate Band

Inheritance Tax is only paid on the value of the transfer above a certain threshold. The basic threshold is called the "Nil Rate Band" and is currently set at £325,000.

There is also an additional threshold known as the "Residence Nil Rate Band".

The Residence Nil Rate Band:

1. is the lower of:the value of the home or share of the home and £175,000;

2. only applies if part of the assets being transferred on death include the home (or a share of the home) of the individual who has died;

3. only applies if this is passed on to a direct descendant, who is defined as:

    3.1. a child or their descendants (i.e. grandchild, great grandchild etc)

    3.2. a stepchild or their descendants

    3.3. an adopted child or their descendants

    3.4. a child of which the deceased was appointed a guardian when the child was under 18

    3.5. a spouse or a civil partner of any of the above;

4. only applies in full if the total value of the deceased's estate is £2,000,000 or less (reducing on a sliding scale where the estate is between £2,000,000 and £2,350,000;

5. cannot be claimed if the total value of the estate is £2,350,000 or more.

# Chapter 18: Basic Inheritance Tax Calculations

### Example 15 - Married Couple, £1.9 Million Estate

John and Mary Brown have the following assets:

| | |
|---|---|
| Home | £500,000 |
| Property Portfolio | £900,000 |
| Investments | £400,000 |
| Cash | £50,000 |
| Furniture & Sundry Possessions | £50,000 |
| **Total Estate** | **£1,900,000** |

Neither John nor Mary have gifted anything to anyone, other than "normal" gifting such as birthday and Christmas presents.

When John dies, Mary inherits everything. There is no Inheritance Tax due on transfers between spouses, so there is no Inheritance Tax on John's death.

As John transferred everything to Mary he has not used his allowances (the Nil Rate Band and the Residence Nil Rate Band). Mary therefore inherits those allowances and can add them to her own to offset against the value of her estate on her death.

When Mary dies, assuming no change in values, the Inheritance Tax calculation is as follows:

| | |
|---|---|
| Total Estate | £1,900,000 |
| | |
| Mary's Nil Rate Band | £325,000 |
| Mary's Residence Nil Rate Band | £175,000 |
| Nil Rate Band inherited from John | £325,000 |
| Residence Nil Rate Band inherited from John | £175,000 |
| Total Allowances | £1,000,000 |
| | |
| Taxable Estate | £900,000 |
| | |
| Inheritance Tax @ 40% | £360,000 |
| | |
| **Total Estate** | **£1,900,000** |
| Less Inheritance Tax | £360,000 |
| **Net Estate after Tax** | **£1,540,000** |

John and Mary's children have to pay £360,000 Inheritance Tax before they can receive any of the net balance of £1,540,000 from their parents' estate. HMRC has to receive its £360,000 first, and the estate is frozen until this is paid.

## Example 16 - Married Couple, £4 Million Estate

Brian and Anne Green have the following assets:

| | |
|---|---:|
| Home | £1,000,000 |
| Property Portfolio | £1,600,000 |
| Investments | £1,250,000 |
| Cash | £75,000 |
| Furniture & Sundry Possessions | £75,000 |
| **Total Estate** | **£4,000,000** |

Neither Brian nor Anne have gifted anything to anyone, other than "normal" gifting such as birthday and Christmas presents.

When Brian dies he passes everything on to Anne. There is no Inheritance Tax due on transfers between spouses, so there is no Inheritance Tax on Brian's death.

As Brian transferred everything to Anne he has not used his Nil Rate Band allowance. Anne therefore inherits this allowance and can add it to her own to offset against the value of her estate on her death.

There are no Residence Nil Rate Band allowances, as neither of their estates were below the threshold for this at the time of death.

When Anne dies, assuming no change in values, the Inheritance Tax calculation is as follows:

| | | |
|---|---|---|
| Total Estate | | £4,000,000 |
| | | |
| Anne's Nil Rate Band | | £325,000 |
| Nil Rate Band inherited from Brian | | £325,000 |
| Total Allowances | | £650,000 |
| | | |
| Taxable Estate | £3,350,000 | |
| | | |
| Inheritance Tax @ 40% | £1,340,000 | |
| | | |
| **Total Estate** | **£4,000,000** | |
| Less Inheritance Tax | £1,340,000 | |
| **Net Estate after Tax** | **£2,660,000** | |

Brian and Anne's children have to pay £1,340,000 Inheritance Tax before they can receive any of the net balance of £2,660,000 from their parents' estate. HMRC has to receive its £1,340,000 first, and the estate is frozen until this is paid.

## Comparison of Examples 15 and 16

Even though Brian and Anne's estate was £2,100,000 more than John and Mary's, their children only received an additional £1,120,000. This is because more of the estate was taxable, due to the loss of the Residence Nil Rate Band.

With some straightforward planning, Brian and Anne could have retained the Residence Nil Rate Band and passed an additional £140,000 on to their children.

The use of a number of the strategies outlined later in this book could not only have reduced the Inheritance Tax liability by £140,000 but could have removed the liability altogether:

- saving John and Mary's family £360,000
- saving Brian and Anne's family £1,340,000.

# Chapter 19: Generational Inheritance Tax

Inheritance Tax is charged each time assets are passed on to the next generation. Over a number of generations this can mean your family gets virtually nothing, as most of what you owned ends up in the hands of the tax man.

Each time your assets are passed to the next generation another 40% is taken by HM Revenue & Customs. This is what we call "Generational Inheritance Tax".

This depletion of your assets continues each time they pass on to the next generation unless you take steps to stop it happening.

If your children have a taxable estate of their own, anything you pass on directly to them will be taxed at 40% if they then pass it on to their children, i.e. your grandchildren.

This might more easily be explained with an example.

## Example 17 – £1,500,000 through 2 Generations

Alan and Margaret Black have an estate of £1,500,000 which they want to pass on to their children and, ultimately, their grandchildren.

Alan and Margaret's children have their own assets which exceed the Nil Rate and Residence Nil Rate Bands, and so everything they inherit from their parents will suffer Inheritance Tax.

Alan dies first.

| | | |
|---|---|---|
| Total Estate | £1,500,000 | |
| Margaret's Nil Rate Band | | £325,000 |
| Margaret's Residence Nil Rate Band | | £175,000 |
| Nil Rate Band inherited from Alan | | £325,000 |
| Residence Nil Rate Band inherited from Alan | | £175,000 |
| Total Allowances | | £1,000,000 |
| Taxable Estate | £500,000 | |
| Inheritance Tax @ 40% | £200,000 | |
| **Total Estate** | **£1,500,000** | |
| Less Inheritance Tax | £200,000 | |
| **Net Estate for their Children** | **£1,300,000** | |
| Less Inheritance Tax | £520,000 | |
| **Net Estate for their Grandchildren** | **£780,000** | |

**Total Inheritance Tax paid by Children & Grandchildren   £720,000**

It is easier to reduce or even stop Generational Inheritance Tax than controlling Inheritance Tax in the first generation. What is required is advance planning.

# Chapter 20: Lifetime Transfers

Inheritance Tax is not just payable on the value of a person's assets at their death. Transfers made during a person's lifetime also have Inheritance Tax implications.

**Example 18 - Lifetime Gift 3 Years before Death**

As an example of this, consider the case of John and Mary Brown (Chapter 18 Example 15).

As a reminder here was their Inheritance Tax calculation on Mary's death (after John's earlier death):

| | |
|---|---|
| Total Estate | £1,900,000 |
| | |
| Mary's Nil Rate Band | £325,000 |
| Mary's Residence Nil Rate Band | £175,000 |
| Nil Rate Band inherited from John | £325,000 |
| Residence Nil Rate Band inherited from John | £175,000 |
| Total Allowances | £1,000,000 |
| | |
| Taxable Estate | £900,000 |
| | |
| Inheritance Tax @ 40% | £360,000 |
| | |
| **Total Estate** | **£1,900,000** |
| Less Inheritance Tax | £360,000 |
| **Net Estate after Tax** | **£1,540,000** |

But now let's imagine Mary had gifted £100,000 to their children three years before her death.

If this were the case, **the Inheritance Tax on her death would increase by £40,000 to £400,000. The net estate** passed on to her children **would therefore be reduced by £40,000 to £1,500,000.**

Timing can be so important when planning for Inheritance Tax!

## Chapter 21: Exempt Transfers

Anything you give to your spouse or civil partner is immediately exempt from Inheritance Tax, provided they are UK domiciled. That is, there is no Inheritance Tax to pay because of the gift. The estate of your spouse or civil partner is, of course, increased by the gift, and therefore this has Inheritance Tax implications on their death.

Gifts to charities are also immediately exempt from Inheritance Tax.

Finally, there is an HM Revenue & Customs defined list of other circumstances in which a gift is exempt from Inheritance Tax. Please see later in this book for more information on these exempt transfers.

# Chapter 22: Potentially Exempt Transfers (PETs)

If you give assets away to individuals there is no Inheritance Tax to pay at the time of the gift. However, those assets are still counted as part of your taxable estate for Inheritance Tax until 7 years after the gift. Such gifts are known as "Potentially Exempt Transfers", or "PETs", as they have the potential of being exempt from Inheritance Tax but are not immediately exempt. You must survive 7 years from the gift to obtain the exemption.

There is no limitation at all on the amount you can give away that qualifies as a PET. You could, for example, give your children the full value of your estate above the Nil Rate Band so that when you die (if this is at least 7 years after the gift) they will not have to pay any Inheritance Tax at all.

You should note that the definition of a PET includes the words *"gift to another individual"*. A company is *not* an individual, and therefore **a gift to a company is *not* potentially exempt from Inheritance Tax.** See the next chapter for more on this.

Forgiving a debt is regarded as a gift for this purpose, and therefore the moment the debt is forgiven the 7 year "PET clock" begins.

*Taper Relief on PETs*

If you die during the first 2 years following the gift your estate will have to pay 40% Inheritance Tax on the amount gifted.

If you die between 2 and 7 years following the gift, the whole value of the gift is added back to your estate to assess the Inheritance Tax due, but the tax payable on the gift is reduced. The tax payable is as follows:

| Months from death | Tax |
|---|---|
| 0 to 24 | 40% |
| 25 to 36 | 32% |
| 37 to 48 | 24% |
| 49 to 60 | 16% |
| 61 to 72 | 8% |
| 73 onwards | 0% |

## Example 19 - Gift 1 Year before Death

Consider again the example of Mary Brown (Chapter 18, example 12). Mary's husband, John, died a few years before her, leaving his entire estate to Mary.

If there had been no lifetime gifts, as shown in Chapter 18, the Inheritance Tax and the estate passed on to Mary's children would have been as follows:

| | | |
|---|---|---|
| Total Estate | | £1,900,000 |
| Mary's Nil Rate Band | | £325,000 |
| Mary's Residence Nil Rate Band | | £175,000 |
| Nil Rate Band inherited from John | | £325,000 |
| Residence Nil Rate Band inherited from John | | £175,000 |
| Total Allowances | | £1,000,000 |
| Taxable Estate | £900,000 | |
| Inheritance Tax @ 40% | £360,000 | |
| **Total Estate** | **£1,900,000** | |
| Less Inheritance Tax | £360,000 | |
| **Net Estate after Tax** | **£1,540,000** | |

Mary, however, gave £100,000 to her children a year before she died.

The Inheritance Tax and the estate passed on to Mary's children is now:

| | | |
|---|---|---|
| Total Estate | | £1,900,000 |
| Mary's Nil Rate Band | | £325,000 |
| Mary's Residence Nil Rate Band | | £175,000 |
| Nil Rate Band inherited from John | | £325,000 |
| Residence Nil Rate Band inherited from John | | £175,000 |
| Total Allowances | | £1,000,000 |
| Taxable Estate | £900,000 | |
| Inheritance Tax @ 40% on Estate | £360,000 | |
| Lifetime Gift | | £100,000 |
| Inheritance Tax @ 40% on Gift | £40,000 | |
| Total Inheritance Tax | £400,000 | |
| **Total Estate** | **£1,900,000** | |
| Less Inheritance Tax | £400,000 | |
| **Net Estate after Tax** | **£1,500,000** | |

The children therefore receive £40,000 less because of the gift she made the year before she died.

In this example the children are no worse off than if she had not given them £100,000 the year before she died, as they now have that gift.

They are no better off than if she had not given this to them, though, as the Inheritance Tax on the gift is 40%. Mary may have given them the gift in the hope that this would reduce the Inheritance Tax on her death, but this is not the case. The gift was a "Potentially Exempt Gift", and in this case the "potential" exemption was not realised because Mary died too soon for that to be the case.

If she had made the gift to someone other than her children, they are now worse off because of that gift even though they did not benefit from it. Not only has someone else benefitted from the gift, but also, they have now received £40,000 less because of the Inheritance Tax on a gift they didn't even receive.

## Example 20 - Gift 4 Years before Death

If, instead, Mary had given her children the £100,000 four years before her death, the additional Inheritance Tax would be 24% on the gift, and the calculation would be as follows:

| | |
|---|---|
| Total Estate | £1,900,000 |

| | |
|---|---|
| Mary's Nil Rate Band | £325,000 |
| Mary's Residence Nil Rate Band | £175,000 |
| Nil Rate Band inherited from John | £325,000 |
| Residence Nil Rate Band inherited from John | £175,000 |
| Total Allowances | £1,000,000 |
| | |
| Taxable Estate | £900,000 |
| | |
| Inheritance Tax @ 40% on Estate | £360,000 |
| Lifetime Gift | £100,000 |
| Inheritance Tax @ 24% on Gift | £24,000 |
| Total Inheritance Tax | £384,000 |
| | |
| **Total Estate** | **£1,900,000** |
| Less Inheritance Tax | £384,000 |
| **Net Estate after Tax** | **£1,516,000** |

The children therefore receive £24,000 less because of the gift she made four years before she died.

### Example 21 - Gift 7 Years before Death

If, instead, Mary had given her children the £100,000 seven years before her death, there would be no additional Inheritance Tax on the gift, and the calculation would be as follows:

| | |
|---|---|
| Total Estate | £1,900,000 |

| | |
|---|---|
| Mary's Nil Rate Band | £325,000 |
| Mary's Residence Nil Rate Band | £175,000 |
| Nil Rate Band inherited from John | £325,000 |
| Residence Nil Rate Band inherited from John | £175,000 |
| Total Allowances | £1,000,000 |

| | | |
|---|---|---|
| Taxable Estate | £900,000 | |
| | | |
| Inheritance Tax @ 40% on Estate | £360,000 | |
| Lifetime Gift | | £100,000 |
| Inheritance Tax @ 0% on Gift | £0 | |
| Total Inheritance Tax | £360,000 | |

| | |
|---|---|
| **Total Estate** | **£1,900,000** |
| Less Inheritance Tax | £360,000 |
| **Net Estate after Tax** | **£1,540,000** |

The children therefore do not receive any less because of the gift she made seven years before she died. This would also be the case if she made it eight years or any other greater number of years before she died.

# Chapter 23: Chargeable Lifetime Transfers

If you give away assets other than to an individual this is a "Chargeable Lifetime Transfer". A gift to a disabled person's trust is a Potentially Exempt Transfer (see previous chapter).

When you make a Chargeable Lifetime Transfer you must pay 20% Inheritance Tax soon after the time of the transfer.

If you die within 7 years of the transfer your estate, then has to pay another 20% Inheritance Tax on the transfer.

## Note 1

As with Inheritance Tax on death you benefit first from the Nil Rate Band, so you only pay the tax if your total transfers exceed this. Chargeable Lifetime Transfers do *not* benefit from the Residence Nil Rate Band.

## Note 2

There is never any refund of the 20% Lifetime Charge, even if on death the estate is below the Nil Rate Band.

## Note 3

The Nil Rate Band is reduced by the total of any transfers you have made within the last 7 years. If you make several transfers in a 7 year period you may therefore have to pay the 20% tax even though none of those transfers exceed the Nil Rate Band – it is the total of all such transfers that counts.

### Example 22 – Chargeable Lifetime Transfer

David and Sarah White have a total estate of £3 million. They have talked with a "knowledgeable friend" about Inheritance Tax and know that because of the size of their estate they will not benefit from the Residence Nil Rate Band (see Chapter 17) and there will therefore be more Inheritance Tax on their estate than would otherwise be the case.

The calculation is:

| | | |
|---|---|---|
| Total Estate | | £3,000,000 |
| | | |
| Sarah's Nil Rate Band | | £325,000 |
| Nil Rate Band inherited from David | | £325,000 |
| Total Allowances | | £650,000 |
| | | |
| Taxable Estate | | £2,350,000 |
| | | |
| Inheritance Tax @ 40% | | £940,000 |
| | | |
| **Total Estate** | | **£3,000,000** |
| Less Inheritance Tax | | £940,000 |
| **Net Estate after Tax** | | **£2,060,000** |

In this example we have assumed David dies first, so Sarah inherits David's Nil Rate Band, but the calculation is the same if Sarah dies first and David inherits Sarah's Nil Rate Band.

David and Sarah make a chargeable lifetime transfer of £1 million, bringing their estate down to £2 million. An estate of £2 million or less can benefit from the Residence Nil Rate Band, so this should reduce the Inheritance Tax.

They have worked out the calculation is now:

| | |
|---|---|
| Total Estate | £2,000,000 |

| | |
|---|---|
| Sarah's Nil Rate Band | £325,000 |
| Sarah's Residence Nil Rate Band | £175,000 |
| Nil Rate Band inherited from David | £325,000 |
| Residence Nil Rate Band inherited from David | £175,000 |
| Total Allowances | £1,000,000 |
| | |
| Taxable Estate | £1,000,000 |
| | |
| Inheritance Tax @ 40% | £400,000 |
| | |
| **Total Estate** | **£2,000,000** |
| Less Inheritance Tax | £400,000 |
| **Net Estate after Tax** | **£1,600,000** |

There is Inheritance Tax here of £400,000 compared with the Inheritance Tax of £940,000 if they had not made the transfer. So they believe there is a tax saving of £540,000.

But that is not the case.

For the purpose of our calculations, we will assume they each made a chargeable lifetime transfer of £500,000. When they made this transfer they first offset the £325,000 Nil Rate Band, leaving a taxable lifetime transfer of £175,000. There is an immediate Inheritance Tax bill to be paid on this of £35,000.

Here are the calculations:

| | |
|---|---|
| Lifetime Gift | £500,000 |
| less Nil Rate Band | £325,000 |
| Taxable Lifetime Gift | £175,000 |
| | |
| Inheritance Tax @ 20% on Gift | £35,000 |

This is on each of the two £500,000 gifts, so in total they have had to pay £70,000. This must be paid immediately, not simply when they die.

So the saving is £470,000, not £540,000 (i.e. the £540,000 saving on death, as outlined above, less the immediate payment of £70,000 when they made the gifts).

But this all assumes David and Sarah survive 7 years from the date of the transfers. If they do not, the calculation will be quite different.

In this calculation we have again assumed David dies first, but again the figures will be the same whether David or Sarah is the first to die. The only difference is in which Nil Rate Band is the "inherited Nil Rate Band".

Here is the new calculation of Inheritance Tax assuming both David and Sarah die within 7 years of their gifts:

| | | |
|---|---|---|
| Total Estate | | £2,000,000 |
| | | |
| Mary's Residence Nil Rate Band | | £175,000 |
| Residence Nil Rate Band inherited from David | | £175,000 |
| Total Allowances | | £350,000 |
| | | |
| Taxable Estate | | £1,650,000 |
| | | |
| Inheritance Tax @ 40% on Estate | | £660,000 |
| Inheritance Tax @ 20% on Gift | | £70,000 |
| Total Inheritance Tax | | £730,000 |
| | | |
| **Total Estate** | | **£2,000,000** |
| Less Inheritance Tax | | £730,000 |
| **Net Estate after Tax** | | **£1,270,000** |

There is no Nil Rate Band for either Mary or David as they both used up all their Nil Rate Bands when they made their lifetime gifts.

**Total Inheritance Tax Paid**
| | |
|---|---|
| On gifts at time of gift | £70,000 |
| At time of death | £730,000 |
| **Total** | **£800,000** |

They have therefore paid a total of £800,000 Inheritance Tax if you add the tax paid at the time of the gift to the tax paid on death. This compares with £940,000 they would have paid if they had not taken any action. This is a saving of £140,000, which is much less than the £540,000 they thought they were going to save!

## Chapter 24: Gifts with Reservation of Benefit

Any assets you give away will still be regarded as owned by you when Inheritance Tax is calculated, unless you can clearly show that you no longer gain any benefits from those assets.

When you cannot show that you no longer gain any benefits from assets you have given away, those gifts are called "Gifts with Reservation of Benefit".

### Note 1

A Gift with Reservation of Benefit is still a true gift even though for Inheritance Tax purposes it is treated as if it still belonged to the donor. As it is a true gift this means the donor cannot demand its return and assume the person who received it must give it back.

## Note 2

Just as HM Revenue & Customs can decide that a gift is not really a gift for Inheritance Tax purposes, so can creditors. If there is enough evidence for the Revenue to decide it effectively still belongs to the donor, almost certainly any creditors could reach the same conclusion.

For example, if the donor requires long term care, the local authority is very likely to rule that such a gift was a "deliberate deprivation of assets" and take its value into account when working out how much the individual must pay towards the care costs.

## Note 3

If the person who receives a gift sells that gift and makes a capital gain, the Capital Gains Tax calculation will go back to the date they received the gift. Even though it is now treated as a Gift with Reservation of Benefit, and Inheritance Tax was paid on the death of the donor, the capital gain within the asset remains and is not extinguished by the death.

If the donor had simply kept the asset and not given it away, on the donor's death any capital gain within the asset would be extinguished by the death.

By giving the asset away in a way in which HM Revenue & Customs can apply the "Gifts with Reservation of Benefit" rules, the donor has therefore ensured that both Inheritance Tax and Capital Gains tax apply, and therefore increased the tax burden.

## Example 23 - Gift of Holiday Home to Daughter

Bridget Jones has a holiday home on the coast. As she takes fewer holidays than she used to enjoy she decides to give the holiday home to her daughter.

However, every so often Bridget still uses that home for her own holidays. Even though this is not a regular annual visit HM Revenue & Customs still decides that Bridget has retained a benefit in this holiday home. On Bridget's death they rule that the holiday home is part of her estate. Although she gifted it to her daughter this was a Gift with Reservation of Benefit and therefore Inheritance Tax of 40% is charged on the value of the property.

## Example 24 - Gift of own Home to Son

George Bailey's wife died several years ago and he now feels he is rattling around on his own in a big house he no longer really needs. His son and daughter-in-law, Harry & Emily, do not own their own house and live in a rental property. George therefore gives his house away to Harry.

George continues to live in the house, but pays Harry a small rent. The rent is one which George and Harry consider reasonable, but they have kept it quite low so that it does not result in too much of an income tax charge for Harry.

On George's death HM Revenue & Customs decide that the rent he was paying was not a true market rent. They therefore treat his gift of the house to George as a Gift with Reservation, and therefore the house is added back into the estate for the calculation of Inheritance Tax.

## Example 25 - Gift of Painting to Brother

Jack Carlson is very wealthy and knows there will be a large Inheritance Tax bill on his estate before his children can inherit. His brother, William, however, is worth around £100,000 and therefore there will be no Inheritance Tax on William's estate.

Jack owns a painting worth around £200,000. If he gives this to William this should reduce the Inheritance Tax on Jack's estate by £80,000, but the addition of £200,000 to William's estate will still not bring the value of that estate above the Nil Rate Band, so it will not add an Inheritance Tax liability to William's estate.

This seems to Jack to be a perfect solution, so he gives the painting to William.

As Jack and William live quite close, Jack visits his brother quite often, of course. This means he can still enjoy looking at the painting. HM Revenue & Customs can readily argue that the gift of the painting to William was a Gift with Reservation, and that its value should be added to Jack's estate when Inheritance Tax is calculated.

## Chapter 25: Pre-owned Assets Tax

On the suggestion of HM Revenue & Customs, Parliament has put in place an anti-avoidance measure which charges tax if you give away an asset and then change your mind and take it back. It is intended to stop people using "clever" schemes to avoid paying Inheritance Tax on anything that benefits them but which is not classed as a "Gift with Reservation of Benefit". But it applies in many cases where there was no attempt to avoid Inheritance Tax and a person's circumstances have simply changed and mean they need to take back whatever they gave away.

This anti-avoidance measure is called the "Pre-owned Asset Tax", and it is charged as Income Tax on whatever was given away.

Pre-owned Assets Tax is charged on a reasonable value of "rent" for the asset, times your marginal rate of Income Tax. Around 6% might be a typical rental yield on a property, so the Pre-owned Assets Tax would be your marginal Income Tax rate (say 40%) on 6% of the value you gave away.

Where it is not possible to state a reasonable value of rent, or where the benefit received is a gift of money, HM Revenue & Customs would normally use their official rate of interest for "beneficial loan arrangements". At the time this book was written, the last published HMRC official rate of interest was 2%.

## Example 26 - Gifted House Taken Back & Lived In

Fred Smith owns an investment property. His son needs somewhere to live, so Fred gives him the property.

Many years later, Fred's situation changes. With his son's agreement he moves into the property and lives in it. Fred is a 40% taxpayer.

Fred now has to pay Pre-Owned Asset Tax on the rental value of the property (at the value at the time he gave it away, not its value now).

Here is the calculation of the annual tax due:

| | |
|---|---|
| Property given away | £500,000 |
| Rental value | 6% |
| Notional Annual Rent | £30,000 |
| Fred's Marginal Tax Rate | 40% |
| Income Tax | £12,000 |

Fred therefore must pay Income Tax of £12,000 every year until he stops living in the house.

The £500,000 here is the original value of the property, not the value at the time Fred takes it back.[2] It may be worth £1,000,000 now, but the tax calculation is based on that original value, not its current value.

## Example 27 - Gifted House Taken Back & Sold

Agnes Carter owns an investment property. Her daughter needs somewhere to live, so Agnes gives her the property.

Many years later, with her daughter's agreement, Agnes takes the property back and sells it. She uses the cash proceeds to pay for her ongoing cost of living. Agnes is a 20% taxpayer.

Agnes now must pay Pre-Owned Asset Tax on the rental value of the property (at the value at the time she gave it away, not its value now).

Here is the calculation of the annual tax due:

| | |
|---|---|
| Property given away | £400,000 |
| Rental value | 6% |
| Notional Annual Rent | £24,000 |
| Agnes's Marginal Tax Rate | 20% |
| Income Tax | £4,800 |

---

[2] Technically the calculation dictated by HM Revenue & Customs uses the current value of the asset. But as you then multiply this by the fraction of its value at the time it was gifted over its current value, the overall effect is the same as if you simply used the original value.

Agnes therefore has to pay Income Tax of £4,800 every year until either she dies or repays her daughter £400,000 to give her back the value she originally gave to her.

As in the previous example, the £400,000 used for the tax calculation is the original value of the property, not the value at the time Agnes takes it back.

## Comparison of Examples 26 and 27

In Example 25, Fred lived in the property when he took it back and had to pay Income Tax on this benefit for as long as he lived there.

In Example 26 Agnes did not live in the property, but as she used the cash from the sale of the property she had to pay Income Tax on this benefit for the rest of her life, unless she paid her daughter back.

In both these examples there are also the complications of who is deemed to have owned the property (or the cash from its sale) when Inheritance Tax is calculated on the death of the parent or child.

## Example 28 - Money Gift Taken Back

Helen Lord gives her son £300,000 so he can get his foot on the property ladder.

10 years later Helen's circumstances have changed and her son gives her £250,000 to help.

Helen now must pay Pre-Owned Asset Tax on the £250,000 her son returned to her.

Here is the calculation of the annual tax due:

| | |
|---|---:|
| Money taken back | £250,000 |
| HMRC Official Interest Rate | 2% |
| Notional Annual Rent | £5,000 |
| Helen's Marginal Tax Rate | 20% |
| Income Tax | £1,000 |

Agnes therefore has to pay Income Tax of £1,000 every year until either she dies or repays her son the £250,000 he gave back to her.

## Note 1

If the calculated rental value of the benefit is £5,000 or less there will be no tax charge. This is an "all or nothing" exemption, though, not simply a threshold. If the benefit value exceeds £5,000 the entire benefit will be chargeable, not simply the excess over £5,000.

## Note 2

If you want to avoid the Pre-owned Assets Tax but do not wish to give the asset back, you can apply to HM Revenue & Customs to treat the original gift as a Gift with Reservation of Benefit, which means it is now within your estate for Inheritance Tax, or to enter into a rental agreement with the person who returned your gift and pay the market rent for it. It is not sufficient simply to pay the rent, as there must be a legal obligation to pay it or it will be ignored for Pre-owned Assets Tax purposes.

## Note 3

When you take back an asset you have gifted to someone there are tax implications for that person too. If there was a capital gain on the asset between the time of the gift and when you take it back, the person who received the gift from you may have to pay Capital Gains Tax. Also, even though you have taken the asset back, it is still in the other person's estate for Inheritance Tax purposes until 7 years after you have taken it back.

# Chapter 26: Administration of Inheritance Tax

The people responsible for the administration of an estate are known as "Personal Representatives".

Inheritance Tax is the first debt the Personal Representatives must settle. Until the Inheritance Tax is paid it is not possible to get a Grant of Probate, obtain control of the assets and pass them on to the beneficiaries. This concept dates back to 1881, and makes it easier for HM Revenue & Customs to get their share of the estate.

The Personal Representatives will normally try to pay the Inheritance Tax as soon as possible so that they can gain control of the estate and begin the distribution process, but there is an HM Revenue & Customs deadline of 6 months following the end of the month in which the death occurred. If the tax is not paid by this deadline, interest will accrue.

It is quite common for there to be delays and for interest to accrue, as many estates are complex. A way the Personal Representatives can reduce or avoid this problem is by making a tax return and paying the tax within the 6 month period. They then submit a later correction and pay interest only on the excess if the Inheritance Tax was underpaid.

### Obtaining Funds to Pay Inheritance Tax

The Personal Representatives must pay the Inheritance Tax before they can take control of the assets within the estate, but they need to use assets within the estate to pay the Inheritance Tax. This is rather a classic "catch 22" situation.

There are three possible solutions to this problem:

1. Whilst banks and other financial institutions will not allow Personal Representatives to draw funds to pay the beneficiaries without a Grant of Probate, they will allow them to withdraw fund just to pay the Inheritance Tax.
2. There may be assets in held trust for the benefit of those who will benefit from the deceased's estate, in which case it may be possible to draw on those assets to pay the Inheritance Tax liability. This may be
    2.1. cash paid by an insurance company on the individual's death, or
    2.2. a "Probate Trust" set up by the individual before death so that cash is available without the requirement for Probate.

The Personal Representatives are often the Trustees of any such trusts and can therefore control the funds within them, but if not they could ask the Trustees to make the required payment to HM Customs & Excise.

3. If there is not sufficient money in the estate bank accounts and/or trusts to pay the Inheritance Tax, the Personal Representatives will have to take out a loan to pay it. They will then be personally responsible for repaying the loan.

### Payment by Instalments

It is possible to pay Inheritance Tax in 10 equal annual instalments, but only where the Inheritance Tax relates to qualifying assets. The qualifying assets for instalment payment are:

- Land and property
- A business interest
- Timber (after being left out of account for Inheritance Tax on a previous death – see "Invest in Woodland" in Chapter 24)
- Controlling shareholdings
- Unquoted shares

The first instalment of the 10 year instalment payment plan must be paid no later than 6 months after the end of the month in which the death occurred. HM Revenue & Customs will not agree, for example, to accept the first payment a year after the death.

The instalment option is only available for qualifying assets. This means that there may be 2 tranches of Inheritance Tax to be paid – the amount which can be paid by instalment plan and the amount which must be paid in full right away.

If an asset within the "instalment plan tranche" is sold, this element of the estate passes immediately into the tranche which must be paid in full.

### Note – Liability of Personal Representatives

Personal Representatives are either "Executors" or "Administrators".

Executors are those named in a valid Will as having responsibility for settling the estate.

If there is no Will, the Will is not valid, or the Will cannot be found, a court will issue a "Grant of Letters of Administration" to one or more of those entitled to inherit under the rules of intestacy, and those named in the Letters of Administration are known as Administrators.

A Personal Representative takes on a very onerous responsibility as outlined in Chapter 10. He or she has to ensure the wishes of the deceased and the strict letter of the law are followed, and is personally liable if this does not happen. If there are valid claimants who are not paid the amounts they should be paid they can claim this from the Personal Representative, who is legally obliged to pay them. Both HM Revenue & Customs and charities are renowned for insisting Personal Representatives make good any deficits, regardless of whether or not they can then obtain reimbursement from the estate or beneficiaries. This is a very good reason for private individuals to refuse to act as Personal Representatives and to insist the role is taken on by professionals.

# Section 3 - Strategies

Section 3 details legitimate strategies people successfully use to control their Inheritance Tax, reducing or eliminating it altogether.

What is important is to:

1. stop the Inheritance Tax problem getting worse, and;
2. keep chipping away at the existing liability;

perhaps using a combination of different strategies so that eventually the tax liability disappears completely.

# Chapter 27: Strategies for Reducing Inheritance Tax

There are many ways you can legally reduce your likely Inheritance Tax liability. So many, that Inheritance Tax almost looks like a voluntary tax that you only pay if you want to pay it!

All of the strategies listed are perfectly legal and acceptable strategies which use the relevant legislation in the way Parliament intended.

It is not usually possible to simply take one action and immediately remove your whole Inheritance Tax liability.

In the following pages we have covered 34 Inheritance Tax Control strategies that can be used to reduce or eliminate Inheritance Tax.

When considering any of these strategies always keep in mind what you are trying to achieve in total, and not just the "Inheritance Tax Reduction" element of your strategy. Just because a particular strategy reduces Inheritance Tax it does not necessarily mean it is the right thing for you to do. You should look at it in the round and make sure it is congruent with your overall objectives.

Also bear in mind, as outlined previously, that Inheritance Tax is a complex matter for all but the simplest of estates. There are often interactions with other tax matters which can lay financial traps for the unwary. It is therefore very important to take advice from a specialist before attempting to use any of the outlined strategies.

The first section of each strategy outlines what that strategy is.

Under this, in all but the simplest of strategies, is a "Details" section, giving you more information on the strategy if it is of interest.

Where more in-depth information could be helpful there is then a further "Advanced" section which you can study to get more background on this particular strategy.

# Chapter 28: Reduce the Inheritance Tax Value of Your House

You can reduce the value of your house, just for Inheritance Tax purposes and without actually reducing its value, by setting up trusts and writing your Wills to take advantage of those Trusts.

***Details***

If you share your house with your partner or spouse you should each write your Will to put your own share of the house into trust on your death.

HM Revenue & Customs will accept that when the first of you dies, the share of the house owned by the survivor is worth less than 50% of the value of the whole house. This is because the survivor does not own the house outright, but shares the ownership with the Trust set up by his or her spouse.

The fact that the survivor does not own the house outright does not cause any practical issues for that person, as he or she is the main beneficiary of the Trust that owns the other half. But for Inheritance Tax purposes its value is still reduced.

This strategy reduces Inheritance Tax not only for your children, but also for your grandchildren and all the following generations. See Chapter 6 for a reminder on Generational Inheritance Tax, which is the additional tax this strategy is reducing.

As Nelson Rockefeller said, *"the secret to success is to own nothing but control everything"*. Wealthy families have known this and acted on it for centuries. You, too, can do so, starting with your own house.

### *About Trusts*

Trusts have been used for nearly 1,000 years to protect family wealth.

The wealthiest families in this country have always recognised that there are many threats which could attack their wealth. They keep most of their wealth in trust to protect it from those threats but still retain control over that wealth.

## Example 29 - Half of House Goes into Trust

Kevin and Geraldine Dobbs own their own home which is worth £900,000.

They each set up Trusts and their Wills put their estate, including their share of their home, into trust.

Kevin dies first, and his half of their home, valued at £450,000, goes into trust for the benefit of Geraldine and their children. Geraldine owns the remaining half of their home, again worth £450,000.

For Inheritance Tax purposes, though, HM Revenue & Customs accept that this value should be reduced by 15% to £382,500, which is a reduction of £67,500.

When Geraldine dies, the value of her estate for Inheritance Tax purposes is therefore reduced by £67,500. This means a reduction in Inheritance Tax of £27,000.

Putting each of their halves of their home into trust has therefore saved the estate of Kevin and Geraldine £27,000 of Inheritance Tax, as well as saving Inheritance Tax for their children's estates and the estates of all the future generations.

# Chapter 29: Inheritance Tax Pre-Payment Trust

You make a regular monthly or annual payment into an Inheritance Tax Pre-Payment Trust. When you die, the entire Inheritance Tax bill calculated at the outset is cleared in full, regardless of how much or how little you have so far paid into the Trust. The amount you pay into the Trust will much less than the amount of Inheritance Tax it clears.

***Details***

The amount to invest in the Inheritance Tax Pre-Payment Trust is calculated at the outset. The Trust immediately invests the payments in a life insurance policy calculated to cover the Inheritance Tax liability. On your death, whether this is just after you first invest in the Trust or many years later, the insurance policy pays out into the Trust, which then uses this to clear the Inheritance Tax liability.

The full Inheritance Tax liability is covered immediately. You do not have to wait for two years, or even for seven years, as is the case with many other strategies.

Also, on your death the Trust has the funds immediately available to pay the Inheritance Tax. Those funds are never within your estate for Inheritance Tax purpose, and therefore are not subject to Inheritance Tax.

This strategy also helps address the potential Inheritance Tax problems of your beneficiaries. It is structured in such a way that their own taxable estates are, between them, reduced by the total amount of the Inheritance Tax settled.

It is possible to use this as a "partial strategy" if you wish. For example you could choose to cover 50% of your Inheritance Tax liability in this way.

### Example 30 - Inheritance Tax Pre-Payment Trust

Robert and Carol Farrow have an estate of around £5,000,000. Allowing for two Nil Rate Bands, their taxable estate is around £4,350,000 and therefore they are expecting an Inheritance Tax liability of 40% on this, which is £1,740,000, to arise when they both pass away. Robert is 59 and Carol is 56.

They establish an Inheritance Tax Pre-Payment Trust and put £2,250 a month into the Trust. The Trust invests this in a life insurance policy worth £1,740,000.

When both Robert and Carol have died, the life insurance policy will pay out £1,740,000 into the Trust.

Even if both Robert and Carol die after only having put the first £2,250 into the Trust, the policy will still have the full £1,740,000, which the Trust can now use to settle the Inheritance Tax liability.

In this example Carol would have to live another 64 years, i.e. to age 120, before the amount paid into the Trust equalled the amount the Trust will pay out to settle the tax liability.

# Chapter 30: Reclaim Inheritance Tax You Paid on an Inheritance

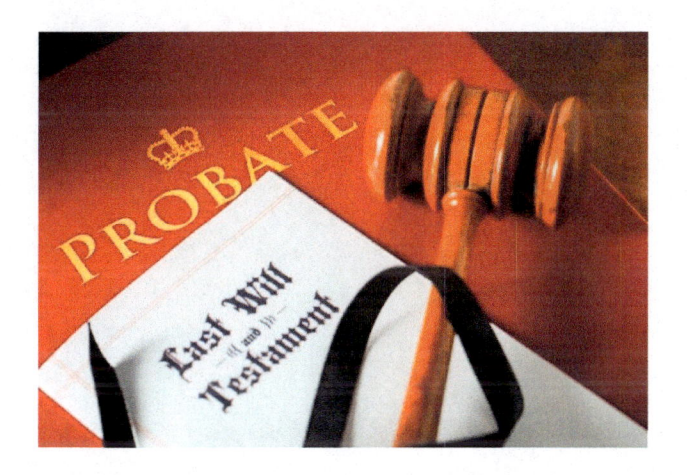

If you are the beneficiary of an estate that has paid more Inheritance Tax than it should, this may be because the person who left this to you received poor advice from a professional. There is a way for you to recover the additional tax the estate paid.

***Details***

It is not uncommon for an adviser without the right level of knowledge and experience to give advice which results in a family paying more Inheritance Tax than they would have paid if the right advice had been given in the first place. As noted, Inheritance Tax is a complex area, so it is not surprising that this should be the case.

The government has put in place a step by step process that allows you to remedy this situation.

# Chapter 31: Change the Tax on an Inheritance You have already Received

If you are left an inheritance and the way in which it was left to you was not tax-efficient, the law allows you to change this to one that is more tax-efficient, i.e. that can reduce Inheritance Tax and Capital Gains Tax.

***Details***

The change will only be effective if it is done within 2 years of the death of the person who left you the inheritance.

It is also only effective if everyone who is affected by the change agrees to it. If you are not trying to receive more than the Will (or the Rules of Intestacy, where there is no valid Will) intended you to receive, this should not normally be a problem. If there are beneficiaries who will not be affected at all by the change you do not need their agreement.

If someone affected by the change is under 18, it will have to be approved by a court, which will have to consider whether it is fully in the interests of the child, and the court will not approve it unless it is certain this is the case.

It is, of course, much better for the planning to be done properly before death. But this option is still there for you to use where pre-death planning is no longer possible.

# Chapter 32: Family Gift Trusts

These are gifts into special trusts, which allow your spouse, children, etc to benefit. These trusts are not subject to Inheritance Tax – i.e. they are Inheritance Tax efficient.

Using Family Gift Trusts alone, over a period of time a couple can double, triple, quadruple their Inheritance Tax free allowance, or even more. This is before using any of the other strategies in this book.

### *Details*

Gifts into a Family Gift Trust will benefit from the Inheritance Tax reduction 7 years after the gift provided you are still alive at that time.

You will not be able to take any benefits from whatever you gift into the trust. Your spouse and children, for example, can take benefits from it, but you cannot.

Your spouse can also gift into a Family Gift Trust from which you can benefit. You and your children, for example, can take benefits from it, but your spouse cannot.

You can put cash into a Family Gift Trust and then have the trust invest it, or you can move property and investments into the trust.

## Example 31 - Recurring Family Gift Trusts

Nigel and Joan Merchant have net assets of around £4,400,000. Their estate is too large for the Residence Nil Rate Band to apply, so they have an Inheritance Tax free allowance of the Nil Rate Band of £325,000 each. They have been informed that **if they take no action there will be an Inheritance Tax bill of £1,500,000 when they die.** Their goal is to reduce this liability.

Nigel puts £325,000 into a Family Gift Trust for the benefit of Joan and their children. Joan puts £325,000 into a Family Gift Trust for the benefit of Nigel and their children.

In 7 years time this effectively means they now have doubled their Inheritance Tax free allowance from £650,000 to £1,300,000.

They now repeat this process at the 7 year mark. Nigel puts another £325,000 into a Family Gift Trust for the benefit of Joan and their children and Joan puts another £325,000 into a Family Gift Trust for the benefit of Nigel and their children.

So in 14 years they have now effectively tripled their Inheritance Tax free allowance to £1,950,000 instead of £650,000.

They repeat this process every 7 years until they die, substantially increasing their Inheritance Tax free allowance each time. So at year 21 they have effectively quadrupled their Inheritance Tax free allowance from £650,000 to £2,600,000. From this strategy alone **they have more than halved the Inheritance Tax liability from £1,500,000 to £720,000.**

By following this strategy, Nigel and Joan have also removed all the growth on the amounts put in trust, reducing the Inheritance Tax on their estate still further. The Inheritance Tax saving from removing this growth, assuming 5% growth per annum, is approximately £850,000, or even more than the saving on removing the capital from the estate.

# Chapter 33: Gift & Loan Trusts

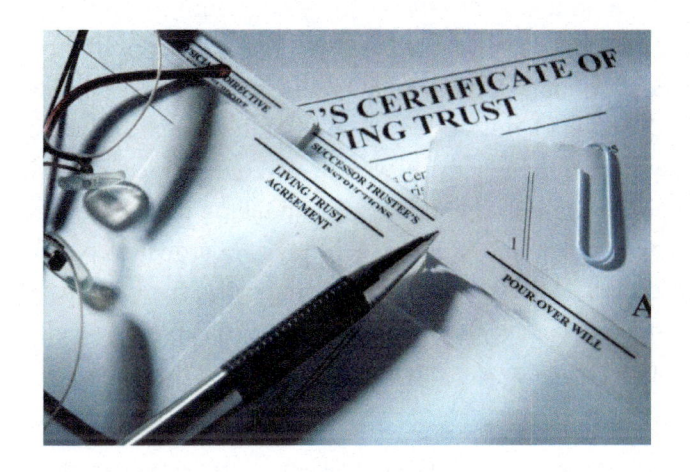

A Gift & Loan Trust freezes the value of part of your estate so the Inheritance Tax liability on this does not get any bigger. It does not reduce the existing Inheritance Tax liability. It is usually used in conjunction with an Inheritance Tax reduction strategy.

With a Gift & Loan Trust you lend money to a trust, the trust then invests it. **All the growth on the gift is outside your estate** for Inheritance Tax purposes, **but the money you have put into the trust is still yours** to enjoy whenever and however you wish.

***Details***

With a Gift & Loan Trust you retain full ownership of the capital you have loaned, but all the growth on the gift is immediately outside your estate and not subject to Inheritance Tax. You can claim back some or all of the capital at any time it is required, although there would, of course, usually be little point in giving it away one month and taking it back the next as there would then presumably be little or no growth kept outside your estate. An exception to this might be where you have an opportunity to make a quick but substantial profit which you want to be outside your estate for Inheritance Tax purposes.

Although you have full access to the original capital value of the gift, you cannot access any of the growth as it is the growth which you have given away.

Typically you would set up a Gift & Loan Trust by making an initial gift of a small sum to "settle" the trust. You would then lend the trust an amount of money – the sum you want to "freeze". The Trust invests this sum, which means all the return on the investment belongs to the Trust, not to you.

### Example 32 - Gift & Loan Trust

Thomas and Denise Robins want to reduce their likely Inheritance Tax liability by around £100,000. They considered giving £250,000 to their children, which would reduce the liability by £100,000 after 7 years, but realised they could not do this as they need the income.

Instead, they invest £1,000 in a Gift & Loan Trust and then lend £250,000 to the Trust. The Trust then invests in a bond.

Every month they take £1,000 <u>tax-free</u> income from the Trust.

After 20 years there is probably still £250,000 in the Trust (from the growth of the bond), but this is completely outside the Inheritance Tax loop. They have continued to benefit from the income they needed, but have still managed to put £250,000 outside their estate for Inheritance Tax and care fee purposes.

- There is no limit at all to the size of loan you can make to a Gift & Loan Trust. In the example there is a £250,000 loan, but it could have been £1 million or more.
- Each Gift & Loan Trust arrangement needs to be bespoke to the individual circumstances. A £250,000 loan was right for Thomas and Denise, but the right amount of loan needs to be determined in each individual case.

# Chapter 34: Discounted Gift Trusts

A Discounted Gift Trust can be used to gain

- an immediate reduction in Inheritance Tax,
- a longer term reduction in Inheritance Tax

but at the same time retain some access to capital.

***Details***

If you want to retain some access to capital but also give it away to reduce your Inheritance Tax, you can make an investment into a Discounted Gift Trust. When you make the gift into the Trust you will agree a pattern of repayments to you of part of the capital over a number of years. This means you can continue to enjoy some benefits from the capital. There will be an immediate reduction in the value of your estate for Inheritance Tax purposes. This will increase over 7 years to the full value of the amount in trust.

## Example 33 - Discounted Gift Trust

Charles Young, who is 60, wants to reduce his taxable estate by £100,000, which would reduce the Inheritance Tax payable by £40,000.

Charles cannot afford to give it all away as he needs the income from it. At the same time he wants an immediate reduction in Inheritance Tax rather than just preventing the liability from increasing.

So Charles invests the £100,000 into a Discounted Gift Trust, with an agreement to withdraw £100 tax-free income every month.

There is an immediate reduction of £80,000[3] in his taxable estate, which is a reduction in Inheritance Tax of £32,000. The remaining £20,000 reduction in the taxable estate will then arise over the following 7 years.

In the meantime, Charles enjoys the tax-free income of £100 a month from the £100,000 investment whilst knowing that he has also reduced the Inheritance Tax liability his beneficiaries will face on his death.

---

[3] Each calculation of the discount in the Inheritance Tax from a Discounted Gift Trust has to be individually agreed at the time of the investment. The quoted £80,000 assumes a healthy individual of this age, slightly rounded down to give a more conservative expectation.

# Comparison of Gift & Loan Trust and Discounted Gift Trusts

1. A Gift & Loan Trust is more flexible than a Discounted Gift Trust but provides less Inheritance Tax benefits.

2. With a Gift & Loan Trust you do not gain an immediate Inheritance Tax benefit. You gain an Inheritance Tax benefit on any growth in the investment. However, with a Discounted Gift Trust you benefit from an immediate reduction in Inheritance Tax.

3. With a Gift & Loan Trust you benefit from the full value of the original capital, but with a Discounted Gift Trust you benefit from an agreed percentage.

4. With a Gift & Loan Trust you can take back whatever you like whenever you like, but with a Discounted Gift Trust you take back the agreed amount of capital in regular tranches, and cannot accelerate or postpone this.

5. Both a Gift & Loan Trust and a Discounted Gift Trust allow you to retain some interest in the capital.

# Chapter 35: Invest in Agricultural Land

There is 100% Inheritance Tax relief on an investment in agricultural land if you personally farm the land. This relief could include your family home. If you own the land but rent it to someone else who farms it, there is 50% Inheritance Tax relief.

*Details*

There is 100% Inheritance Tax relief on the agricultural value of land provided you have personally occupied it for agricultural purposes for at least 2 years. "Agricultural value" may be different from the market value of the land. As Inheritance Tax is payable on market value there may still be Inheritance Tax to pay after this relief.

The land can also include a farmhouse and cottages on the land if they are used in connection with the agricultural purposes. This is often the most attractive feature of Agricultural Property Relief, as this is one of the few situations in which, in the right circumstances, HM Revenue & Customs allow the family home to be passed on without it being assessed for Inheritance Tax.

If you rent the property out to another person to farm and have owned it for at least 7 years, you will get 50% Inheritance Tax relief.

# Chapter 36: Invest in Buildings of Outstanding Interest

If you own a building regarded as being of outstanding interest, provided you follow certain provisions issued by HM Revenue & Customs this asset will be outside your estate for Inheritance Tax purposes. By its very nature this is likely to be a valuable asset, and therefore the Inheritance Tax saving will also be high.

This strategy is usually only worth considering if you believe the beneficiaries are going to keep the property after your death.

### *Details*

Where a building is regarded as being part of our national heritage for historic or architectural reasons, the government wants to encourage its owner to keep and maintain it rather than being forced to sell it to cover tax liabilities.

When considering investing in property, particularly if you intend this investment to be passed down intact to future generations, you may therefore wish to include buildings designated as being of outstanding interest and benefit from this tax advantage.

In order to benefit from the tax relief, the owner of the building has to agree to:

- keep the building properly maintained and in good repair
- allow reasonable access to the public without requiring a prior appointment.

"Reasonable access" does *not* mean the public can enter as and when they wish. The owner can designate certain days and times as "open days" during which members of the public can enter and view the building. The legislation allows the owner to make a reasonable charge for such visits. The owner must publicise the open days and times.

***Advanced***

HM Revenue & Customs decide whether a building is of "outstanding interest" and therefore entitles the owner to Inheritance Tax relief.

If the building is listed in England as Grade I or Grade II or as a Scheduled Monument, or if it is listed as Grade A in Northern Ireland or Scotland, this is a reasonable indication (although not a guarantee) that it will be accepted by HM Revenue & Customs as "Outstanding" for Inheritance Tax purposes.

HM Revenue & Customs takes advice from bodies such as Historic England and Natural England, so confirmation by such a body that a building is of outstanding interest should be powerful evidence in your favour.

Keeping the building maintained and in proper repair is an important requirement for you to be able to obtain Inheritance Tax relief. It is also important to allow the public to view the building on certain days. You are given Inheritance Tax relief in return for maintaining the building and allowing the public to benefit by seeing it.

The relief is withdrawn if the owner does not make those undertakings or does not meet the stated requirements. For this reason, there is a Conditional Exemption from Inheritance Tax.

The way in which the undertakings will be fulfilled needs to be outlined in a Heritage Management Plan.

*Maintenance Trust Fund*

You can set up a Maintenance Fund Trust to provide for maintenance of the building. A Maintenance Fund Trust is exempt from Inheritance Tax.

To protect these tax exemptions, it is important to ensure the amount transferred into a Maintenance Fund Trust is reasonable for the purpose. A transfer of excessive amounts which you cannot demonstrate is appropriate to provide for maintenance of the building could endanger the tax exemption of the Maintenance Fund Trust.

*Public Viewing*

The number of open days in a year depends very much on the nature of the building. As an example, HM Revenue & Customs may require you to open it at least one day a week plus public holidays during spring and summer, resulting in at least 28 open days a year.

It must be open for at least 4 hours between 10 am and 5 pm on an open day.

*Withdrawal of Inheritance Tax relief*

If there is either a serious breach of the undertakings given, or you sell the building (other than by private treaty to one of the bodies listed below), the Inheritance Tax relief is withdrawn. A tax charge will arise at that point.

The amount of Inheritance Tax payable when Inheritance Tax relief is withdrawn is based on the current value of the building rather than the original value at the time the conditional exemption was granted. Capital Gains Tax will also be payable on any gains since the building was either inherited or purchased if the children do not live in it. The Capital Gains Tax you have to pay is deducted from the value of the building before calculating the Inheritance Tax.

Just as an example of the withdrawal of Inheritance Tax relief, imagine you invested £10,000,000 in a Building of Outstanding Value and left this building to your children in your Will. You passed away shortly after buying the building. Your children kept the building, with its Inheritance Tax relief, as an investment and decided not to live in it. After 10 years it has increased in value to £20,000,000. Your children now wish to sell it.

There will be Capital Gains Tax of 28% on the gain of £10,000,000, so a Capital Gains Tax charge of £2,800,000 will arise.

The value of the building for Inheritance Tax purposes will be £20,000,000 less the Capital Gains Tax charge of £2,800,000 – i.e. it will be valued at £17,200,000 for this purpose. There will be 40% Inheritance Tax charge on this discounted value, so the Inheritance Tax charge on the loss of Inheritance Tax relief will be £6,880,000.

The total tax payable on the sale of the building will therefore be £9,680,000 (£2,800,000 Capital Gains Tax and £6,880,000 Inheritance Tax).

Your children will therefore receive £10,320,000 net from the sale of the building worth £20,000,000.

Had you not taken advantage of Inheritance Tax relief, or if your children had decided not to continue taking advantage of it on your death, your children would have paid £4,000,000 Inheritance Tax when they received the building valued at £10,000,000. When they sold it 10 years later for £20,000,000 they would have paid £2,800,000 Capital Gains Tax. The total tax they would have paid would therefore have been £6,800,000, compared with total tax of £9,680,000 if Inheritance Tax relief had still been in place. This is £2,880,000 less tax.

If there were no Inheritance Tax relief, your children would have paid the £4,000,000 Inheritance Tax 10 years earlier than the £6,880,000 they had to pay when Inheritance Tax relief was withdrawn. The Inheritance Tax relief therefore gave them the use of that £4,000,000 over the 10 years before the relief was withdrawn.

This shows it can be quite complex calculating the pros and cons of Inheritance Tax relief if it is later withdrawn. The overall conclusion, though, is that if it is thought the building is likely to remain within the family for at least one generation Inheritance Tax relief is a valuable tax concession, but if there is a reasonable likelihood it will be sold it may not be worth claiming Inheritance Tax relief.

*Sale by Private Treaty*

If you have obtained the benefit of Inheritance Tax relief on a Building of Outstanding Interest but now you or your beneficiaries wish to sell this building, you should always look to do so by private treaty with one of the bodies approved by HM Revenue & Customs. No Inheritance Tax or Capital Gains Tax will then arise.

Naturally the purchaser would expect a substantial discount in the price paid, but this will normally still give you a higher value net than would otherwise have been the case. Typically the purchaser will offer you what you would have received net of both Inheritance Tax and Capital Gains tax if you had sold the building on the open market, plus 10% of the total tax you would otherwise have paid. This is known as a "douceur", which means a "sweetener" for the deal.

Using exactly the same example as above, a property purchased for £10,000,000, passed on to your children who then wish to sell it when it has an open market value of £20,000,000, the likely sale price under a private treaty with an approved body is likely to be calculated as follows:

| | |
|---|---|
| Market Value | £20,000,000 |
| *Less Total Tax on Open Market* | *£9,680,000* |
| Net Value after Tax | £10,320,000 |
| *Plus 10% Douceur* | *£968,000* |

Private Treaty Sale Price      £11,288,000

This is still less than your children would have received if they had not taken advantage of the Inheritance Tax relief, but is certainly better than a sale on the open market where they would have had to pay £9,680,000 tax.

*Approved Bodies for Private Treaty Sales*

The following are bodies which can legally allow you to benefit from a Private Treaty Sale with no Inheritance Tax or Capital Gains Tax:

- The Historic Buildings and Monuments Commission for England
- The National Trust for Places of Historic Interest or Natural Beauty
- The National Trust for Scotland for Places of Historic Interest or Natural Beauty
- The Historic Churches Preservation Trust
- Commission for Rural Communities
- Natural England
- Scottish Natural Heritage
- Any local authority
- Any Government department (including the National Debt Commissioners)
- The Trustees of the National Heritage Memorial Fund
- Countryside Council for Wales
- Any university or university college in the United Kingdom
- A health service body, within the meaning of section 986 of the Corporation Tax Act 2010

# Chapter 37: Invest in Land of Outstanding Beauty or of Historic or Scientific Interest

If you own land regarded as being of outstanding beauty, or of historic or scientific interest, provided you follow certain provisions issued by HM Revenue & Customs this asset will be outside your estate for Inheritance Tax purposes. By its very nature this is likely to be a valuable asset, and therefore the Inheritance Tax saving will also be high.

This strategy is usually only worth considering if you believe the beneficiaries are going to keep the property after your death.

***Details***

Where land is regarded as being part of our national heritage for scenic, historic or scientific reasons, the government wants to encourage its owner to keep and maintain it rather than being forced to sell it in order to cover tax liabilities. It therefore provides Inheritance Tax relief.

When considering investing in land, particularly if you intend this investment to be passed down intact to future generations, you may therefore wish to include land designated as being regarded as being part of our national heritage and benefit from this tax advantage.

In order to benefit from the tax relief the owner of the land has to agree to:

- keep the land properly maintained and in good condition, including protecting any aspects that may be of historic or scientific interest
- allow reasonable access to the public without requiring a prior appointment.

Clearly you would want to keep the land properly maintained and in good condition anyway, for your own purposes, so although this undertaking is a requirement it is not one that should be too concerning. It may also be possible to access public funds to help with this maintenance.

"Reasonable access" does *not* mean the public can enter as and when they wish. The owner can designate certain days and times as "open days" during which members of the public can enter the premises. The legislation allows the owner to make a reasonable charge for such visits. The owner must publicise the open days and times.

***Advanced***

It may not be quite as easy as it is with a land to determine at the outset whether the land will qualify.

The advisers used by HM Revenue and Customs to determine whether or not Inheritance Tax relief should apply are Natural England, the Northern Ireland Environment Agency, Scottish Natural Heritage, and the Countryside Council for Wales.

Keeping the land maintained and in good condition, and protecting any aspects that may be of historic or scientific interest, is an important requirement for you to be able to obtain Inheritance Tax relief. It is also important to allow the public to enjoy the land on certain days. You are given Inheritance Tax relief in return for maintaining the land and allowing the public to benefit by seeing it.

The relief is withdrawn if the owner does not make those undertakings or does not meet the stated requirements. For this reason there is a Conditional Exemption from Inheritance Tax. In this context the "owner" may be an individual, a company, or a trust.

The way in which the undertakings will be fulfilled needs to be outlined in a Heritage Management Plan.

*Maintenance Trust Fund*

You can set up a Maintenance Fund Trust to provide for maintenance and protection of the site.

A Maintenance Fund Trust is exempt from Inheritance Tax.

In order to protect these tax exemptions it is important to ensure the amount transferred into a Maintenance Fund Trust is reasonable for the purpose. A transfer of excessive amounts which you cannot demonstrate is appropriate to provide for maintenance and protection of the site could endanger the tax exemption of the Maintenance Fund Trust.

*Public Viewing*

The number of open days in a year depends very much on the nature of the land. As an example, HM Revenue & Customs may require you to open it at least one day a week plus public holidays during spring and summer, resulting in at least 28 open days a year.

It must be open for at least 4 hours between 10 am and 5 pm on an open day.

*Withdrawal of Inheritance Tax relief*

If there is either a serious breach of the undertakings given, or you sell the land (other than by private treaty to one of the bodies listed below), the Inheritance Tax relief is withdrawn. A tax charge will arise at that point.

The amount of Inheritance Tax payable when Inheritance Tax relief is withdrawn is based on the current value of the land rather than the original value at the time the conditional exemption was granted. Capital Gains Tax will also be payable on any gains since the land was either inherited or purchased. The Capital Gains Tax you have to pay is deducted from the value of the land before calculating the Inheritance Tax, but the total tax bill at that point is still likely to be very high.

Just as an example of the withdrawal of Inheritance Tax relief, imagine you invested £5,000,000 in Land of Outstanding Beauty and left this to your children in your Will. You passed away shortly after buying the land. Your children kept the land, with its Inheritance Tax relief, and after 10 years it has increased in value to £10,000,000. Your children now wish to sell it.

There will be Capital Gains Tax of 20% on the gain of £5,000,000, so a Capital Gains Tax charge of £1,000,000 will arise.

The value of the land for Inheritance Tax purposes will be £10,000,000 less the Capital Gains Tax charge of £1,000,000 – i.e. it will be valued at £9,000,000 for this purpose. There will be 40% Inheritance Tax charge on this discounted value, so the Inheritance Tax charge on the loss of Inheritance Tax relief will be £3,600,000.

The total tax payable on the sale of the land will therefore be £4,600,000 (£1,000,000 Capital Gains Tax and £3,600,000 Inheritance Tax).

Your children will therefore receive £5,400,000 net from the sale of the land worth £10,000,000.

Had you not taken advantage of Inheritance Tax relief, or if your children had decided not to continue taking advantage of it on your death, your children would have paid £2,000,000 Inheritance Tax when they received the land valued at £5,000,000. When they sold it 10 years later for £10,000,000 they would have paid £1,000,000 Capital Gains Tax. The total tax they would have paid would therefore have been £3,000,000, compared with total tax of £4,600,000 if Inheritance Tax relief had still been in place. This is £1,600,000 less tax.

If there were no Inheritance Tax relief, your children would have paid the £2,000,000 Inheritance Tax 10 years earlier than the £3,600,000 they had to pay when Inheritance Tax relief was withdrawn. The Inheritance Tax relief therefore gave them the use of that £2,000,000 over the 10 years before the Relief was withdrawn.

This shows it can be quite complex calculating the pros and cons of Inheritance Tax relief if it is later withdrawn. The overall conclusion, though, is that if it is thought the land is likely to remain within the family for at least one generation Inheritance Tax relief is a valuable tax concession, but if there is a reasonable likelihood it will be sold it may not be worth claiming Inheritance Tax relief.

*Sale by Private Treaty*

If you have obtained the benefit of Inheritance Tax relief on Land of Outstanding Beauty or Historic or Scientific Interest but now you or your beneficiaries wish to sell this land, you should always look to do so by private treaty with one of the bodies approved by HM Revenue & Customs. No Inheritance Tax or Capital Gains Tax will then arise.

Naturally the purchaser would expect a substantial discount in the price paid, but this will normally still give you a higher value net than would otherwise have been the case. Typically the purchaser will offer you what you would have received net of both Inheritance Tax and Capital Gains tax if you had sold the land on the open market, plus 10% of the total tax you would otherwise have paid. This is known as a "douceur", which means a "sweetener" for the deal.

Using exactly the same example as above, a property purchased for £5,000,000, passed on to your children who then wish to sell it when it has an open market value of £10,000,000, the likely sale price under a private treaty with an approved body is likely to be calculated as follows:

| | |
|---|---|
| Market Value | £10,000,000 |
| *Less Total Tax on Open Market* | *£4,840,000* |
| Net Value after Tax | £5,160,000 |
| *Plus 10% Douceur* | *£484,000* |
| Private Treaty Sale Price | £5,644,000 |

This is still less than your children would have received if they had not taken advantage of the Inheritance Tax relief, but is certainly better than a sale on the open market where they would have had to pay £4,840,000 tax.

*Approved Bodies for Private Treaty Sales*

The following are bodies which can legally allow you to benefit from a Private Treaty Sale with no Inheritance Tax or Capital Gains Tax:

- The National Trust for Places of Historic Interest or Natural Beauty
- The National Trust for Scotland for Places of Historic Interest or Natural Beauty
- Commission for Rural Communities
- Natural England
- Scottish Natural Heritage
- Countryside Council for Wales
- The Marine Management Organisation
- The Trustees of the National Heritage Memorial Fund

- The National Endowment for Science, Technology and the Arts
- Any local authority
- Any Government department (including the National Debt Commissioners)
- The Historic Buildings and Monuments Commission for England

# Chapter 38: Invest in Woodland

If you invest in woodland, on your death your beneficiaries can apply for Inheritance Tax relief on the "timber value" of the trees on the land.

***Details***

This could be regarded as a deferral of Inheritance Tax, as the Inheritance Tax which would otherwise have been paid is then added to the tax paid on the sale of the timber.

If the beneficiary dies before the timber is sold, another application can be made for Inheritance Tax relief, deferring it still further.

Given the time it can take for timber to mature this could be a worthwhile strategy. The Inheritance Tax which has not been paid yet, as the timber is still growing, can be invested in other assets (or more woodland), so by the time it is paid one would expect there to have been returns on this deferred tax.

## Example 34 – Woodland Investment

Edwin Hall is 60 years old and his wife Freda is 58. Their son, Leonard, is 33.

Edwin and Freda invest £300,000 in a commercial pine forest. The trees in the forest are around 20 years old and are expected to be harvested in another 20 years.

Edwin and Freda die shortly after buying the forest and have therefore not yet sold the timber. The value of the land and timber on their death is unchanged from when they purchased it.

It is calculated that the value of the timber is £120,000 and the value of the land without the timber is £180,000. There is therefore Inheritance Tax to pay of £72,000 (40% of the land value of £180,000). If they had not invested their £300,000 in commercial timber land the Inheritance Tax would have been £120,000, so the investment has, at that point, saved their estate £48,000 Inheritance Tax.

The value of timber increases at 8% per annum over the next 20 years, so when Leonard harvests the timber he sells it for £590,000. The Inheritance Tax of £48,000 which was saved on his parents' deaths 20 years earlier is now paid, leaving him with £518,000. There is no other tax to pay, as there is no Income Tax, Capital Gains Tax or Corporation Tax on the sale of timber.

Although ultimately the £48,000 Inheritance Tax was therefore paid, on the sale of the timber, this was not until 20 years later. In the meantime Leonard had the use of that £48,000.

In this example we have not allowed for the costs Leonard would have incurred in harvesting and selling the timber, although he may have done all this work himself and saved further costs. But it does illustrate how this Inheritance Tax relief works.

# Chapter 39: Invest in Qualifying Works of Art

If you own a work of art, or a collection of works of art, that is regarded as having "heritage value", provided you follow certain provisions issued by HM Revenue & Customs this will be outside your estate for Inheritance Tax purposes. By its very nature this is likely to be valuable, and therefore the Inheritance Tax saving will also be high.

This strategy is usually only worth considering if you believe the beneficiaries are going to keep the art after your death.

*Details*

"Qualifying Works of Art" has a broad meaning. It includes any pictures, prints, books, manuscripts or other works of art, which are regarded as having "pre-eminent" national, scientific, historic or artistic interest. It also includes collections which are regarded as being of "pre-eminent" national interest as a collection even if the individual works of art within the collection would not so be regarded.

Where a work of art or a collection of art is regarded as being pre-eminent, the government wants to encourage its owner to keep and maintain it rather than being forced to sell it in order to cover tax liabilities. It therefore provides Inheritance Tax relief.

When considering investing in art, particularly if you intend this investment to be passed down intact to future generations, you may therefore wish to include art designated as pre-eminent and benefit from this tax advantage.

In order to benefit from the tax relief the owner of the art has to agree to:

- keep the art safe and in good condition
- allow reasonable access to the public without requiring a prior appointment.

Clearly you would want to keep your art safe and in good condition anyway, for your own purposes, so although this undertaking is a requirement it is not one that should be too concerning. It may also be possible to access public funds to help with this.

"Reasonable access" does *not* mean the public can view your art as and when they wish. You can designate certain days and times as "open days" during which members of the public can view it. The legislation allows the owner to make a reasonable charge for such visits. The owner must publicise the open days and times, and where it can then be viewed.

### *Advanced*

In determining "pre-eminence", HM Revenue & Customs would consult with the Museums, Libraries and Archives Council on whether the work of art falls within any of the following categories:

- It has an especially close association with our history and national life
- As above, but on a more local level
- It is deserving of entry into a national museum or gallery
- It has an important local association and would be deserving of entry into a local museum for this reason
- It is of especial importance for the study of some particular form of art, learning or history
- It has an especially close association with a particular historic setting, for example an important historic building.

Keeping the art safe and in good condition is an important requirement for you to be able to obtain Inheritance Tax relief. It is also important to allow the public to view the art on certain days. You are given Inheritance Tax relief in return for keeping the art safe and in good condition and allowing the public to benefit by viewing it.

The relief is withdrawn if the owner does not make those undertakings or does not meet the stated requirements. For this reason there is a Conditional Exemption from Inheritance Tax. In this context the "owner" may be an individual, a company, or a trust.

*Public Viewing*

The likely public appeal of the work of art is an important factor in determining suitable public access. Vulnerability to the elements, normal location, and the context of that location will also be taken into account.

If the owner's home is suitable to open to the public for viewing the art, this may be one way HM Revenue & Customs would allow the owner to display it, on agreed dates and times. The owner would need to show, though, that the arrangements for display in this way should keep the works of art safe and properly preserved.

The more usual way would be to agree for it to be displayed in an appropriate museum or art gallery during certain periods.

Depending on the nature of the artwork, the owner should be willing if required to lend it to public collections for special exhibitions, and also to provide curators with images to help them in mounting exhibitions.

*Withdrawal of Inheritance Tax relief*

If there is either a serious breach of the undertakings given, or you sell the art (other than by private treaty to one of the bodies listed below), the Inheritance Tax relief is withdrawn. A tax charge will arise at that point.

The amount of Inheritance Tax payable when Inheritance Tax relief is withdrawn is based on the current value of the art work rather than the original value at the time the conditional exemption was granted. Capital Gains Tax will also be payable on any gains since the art was either inherited or purchased. The Capital Gains Tax you have to pay is deducted from the value of the land before calculating the Inheritance Tax.

Just as an example of the withdrawal of Inheritance Tax relief, imagine you invested £1,000,000 in an oil painting and left this to your children in your Will. You passed away shortly after buying the painting. Your children kept the painting, with its Inheritance Tax relief, and after 10 years it has increased in value to £2,000,000. Your children now wish to sell it.

There will be Capital Gains Tax of 20% on the gain of £1,000,000, so a Capital Gains Tax charge of £200,000 will arise.

The value of the painting for Inheritance Tax purposes will be £2,000,000 less the Capital Gains Tax charge of £200,000 – i.e. it will be valued at £1,800,000 for this purpose. There will be 40% Inheritance Tax charge on this discounted value, so the Inheritance Tax charge on the loss of Inheritance Tax relief will be £720,000.

The total tax payable on the sale of the painting will therefore be £920,000 (£200,000 Capital Gains Tax and £720,000 Inheritance Tax).

Your children will therefore receive £1,080,000 net from the sale of the painting worth £2,000,000.

Had you not taken advantage of Inheritance Tax relief, or if your children had decided not to continue taking advantage of it on your death, your children would have paid £400,000 Inheritance Tax when they received the painting valued at £1,000,000. When they sold it 10 years later for £2,000,000 they would have paid £200,000 Capital Gains Tax. The total tax they would have paid would therefore have been £600,000, compared with total tax of £920,000 if Inheritance Tax relief had still been in place. This is £320,000 less tax.

You should note, though, that if there were no Inheritance Tax relief, your children would have paid the £400,000 Inheritance Tax 10 years earlier than the £720,000 they had to pay when Inheritance Tax relief was withdrawn. The Inheritance Tax relief therefore gave them the use of that £400,000 over the 10 years before the Relief was withdrawn.

This shows it can be quite complex calculating the pros and cons of Inheritance Tax relief if it is later withdrawn. The overall conclusion, though, is that if it is thought the painting is likely to remain within the family for at least one generation Inheritance Tax relief is a valuable tax concession, but if there is a reasonable likelihood it will be sold it may not be worth claiming Inheritance Tax relief.

*Sale by Private Treaty*

If you have obtained the benefit of Inheritance Tax relief on a piece of art but now you or your beneficiaries wish to sell this, you should always look to do so by private treaty with one of the bodies approved by HM Revenue & Customs. No Inheritance Tax or Capital Gains Tax will then arise.

Naturally the purchaser would expect a substantial discount in the price paid, but this will still give you a higher value net than would otherwise have been the case. Typically the purchaser will offer you what you would have received net of both Inheritance Tax and Capital Gains tax if you had sold the art work on the open market, plus 25% of the total tax you would otherwise have paid. This is known as a "douceur", which means a "sweetener" for the deal.

Using exactly the same example as above, an oil painting purchased for £1,000,000, passed on to your children who then wish to sell it when it has an open market value of £2,000,000, the likely sale price under a private treaty with an approved body is likely to be calculated as follows:

| | |
|---|---|
| Market Value | £2,000,000 |
| *Less Total Tax on Open Market* | *£920,000* |
| Net Value after Tax | £1,080,000 |
| *Plus 25% Douceur* | *£230,000* |
| Private Treaty Sale Price | £1,310,000 |

This is still less than your children would have received if they had not taken advantage of the Inheritance Tax relief, but is certainly better than a sale on the open market where they would have had to pay £920,000 tax.

*Approved Bodies for Private Treaty Sales*

The following are bodies which can legally allow you to benefit from a Private Treaty Sale with no Inheritance Tax or Capital Gains Tax:

- The National Gallery
- Tate Gallery
- National Portrait Gallery
- British Library
- Victoria and Albert Museum
- Wallace Collection
- The British Museum
- The National Museums of Scotland
- The National Museum of Wales
- The Ulster Museum
- National Museums and Galleries on Merseyside
- The National Art Collections Fund

- Any other similar national institution which exists wholly or mainly for the purpose of preserving for the public benefit a collection of scientific, historic or artistic interest and which is approved for the purposes of this Schedule by the Commissioners for HM Revenue & Customs
- Any museum or art gallery in the United Kingdom which exists wholly or mainly for that purpose and is maintained by a local authority or university in the United Kingdom
- The Friends of the National Libraries
- Imperial War Museum
- Lambeth Palace Library
- London Museum
- National Army Museum
- National Galleries of Scotland
- National Library of Scotland
- National Library of Wales
- National Maritime Museum
- National Postal Museum
- Any library the main function of which is to serve the needs of teaching and research at a university in the United Kingdom
- The Trustees of the National Heritage Memorial Fund
- The National Endowment for Science, Technology and the Arts
- Any university or university college in the United Kingdom
- Any local authority
- Any Government department (including the National Debt Commissioners)

- A health service body, within the meaning of section 986 of the Corporation Tax Act 2010
- Fleet Air Arm Museum

# Chapter 40: Invest in Your Own Trading Business

If you invest in your own business there will be no Inheritance Tax to pay on its value once you have owned it for 2 years.

***Details***

An investment in your own business, as long as it is accepted by HM Revenue & Customs as a trading business rather than an investment business, attracts Business Relief once you have owned it for 2 years. This applies whether you have incorporated your business as a company, trade as a sole trader, or own the business with someone else as a partnership.

Business Relief means that you have no Inheritance Tax to pay even though the value of the business is within your estate. This means you can obtain any benefits you wish from the business without jeopardising the Inheritance Tax relief.

***Advanced***

*Restricting Business Relief*

Business Relief is only available on a business intended to make a profit. If you own a not-for-profit organisation this will not qualify for Business Relief and your estate will have to pay Inheritance Tax on its full value.

This relief is not available if the main purpose of the business is to deal in securities, stocks or shares, land or buildings, or to make or hold investments. If, though, the business is mainly involved in trading but also has some investment activity the entire business will qualify for Business Relief.

Business Relief is not available, though, on assets held within the business but not required for the purpose of the business. These assets are called "excepted assets", and their value is added back to the taxable estate for Inheritance Tax purposes. For example, if your company holds a large cash balance it may be required to show why the business needed such a large balance of cash. If it cannot show why this is needed, the excess cash balance will be an excepted asset. Where you are keeping a large amount of cash or investments in the company for a clearly defined future need, for example to replace some machinery, it is advisable to have this clearly noted in, for example, board meeting minutes, so this can be provided as proof of the need for the cash or investments if such proof is ever required.

*Sale of the Business*

If there is a binding contract of sale of the business at the time of the owner's death this means Business Relief no longer applies and the full value of the business will be charged to Inheritance Tax. It is therefore very important that if your Shareholders' Agreement has a requirement for a widow or widower of a shareholder to sell inherited shares this could not be defined as a binding contract of sale. Such an agreement should be worded as a double option agreement instead.

# Chapter 41: Invest in Unquoted Shares

If you invest in shares that are not quoted on the main stock exchange there will be no Inheritance Tax to pay on their value once you have owned them for 2 years.

*Details*

An investment in a qualifying company that is not quoted on the main stock exchange attracts "Business Relief" in exactly the same way as does your own company. There will be no Inheritance Tax once you have owned it for 2 years, even though you retain full ownership of the shares and can benefit from the capital and any income it produces.

This includes AIM shares, even though they are quoted shares, as they are not quoted on the main stock exchange.

*Advanced*

This relief is not available if the main purpose of the business is to deal in securities, stocks or shares, land or buildings, or to make or hold investments. If, though, the business is mainly involved in trading but also has some investment activity the entire business will qualify for Business Relief.

# Chapter 42: Invest in EIS Shares or Portfolios

If you invest in EIS shares or portfolios of EIS shares there will be no Inheritance Tax to pay on their value once you have owned them for 2 years.

*Details*

An investment in an EIS or an EIS portfolio attracts "Business Relief" in exactly the same way as does an investment in any other unquoted qualifying share. There will be no Inheritance Tax to pay once you have owned it for 2 years, even though you retain full ownership of the shares and can benefit from the capital and any income it produces.

Although, by its nature, an EIS portfolio is riskier than a unit trusts or investment trust, it works in a similar way, allowing you to spread your investment (and therefore risk) over a number of shares.

It also has other significant tax advantages:

- Income Tax relief on the amount invested

- No Capital Gains Tax on any growth in the investment
- Deferral of any capital gains you may have made on other investments (e.g. a sale of properties in a property portfolio)

***Advanced***

As long as you are not connected with the company (i.e. not an employee, director, or a substantial shareholder) you can obtain Income Tax relief of 30% on any investment in an EIS or EIS portfolio. The maximum investment which qualifies for this purpose in a "standard EIS" is £1,000,000, which would give you £300,000 Income Tax relief provided you had an Income Tax liability of that size. The limit is increased to £2,000,000, giving you up to £600,000 Income Tax relief, if the EIS is accepted by HM Revenue & Customs as one which is "knowledge-intensive". You must hold the EIS shares for at least three years, or the Income Tax relief will be clawed back.

If you die within the three years "clawback" period, there is no clawback of the Income Tax relief you received again.

You can sell your EIS shares after three years without losing the original Income Tax relief, and then invest in more EIS shares, gaining Income Tax relief all over again! There is no limit to the number of times you can repeat this. Many EIS investors regard their investment as one which gains 10% every year (i.e. 30% every 3 years when they sell and reinvest in another EIS) before taking any account of the actual growth in their portfolio.

If the EIS is what is defined as a SEIS, which is a smaller company setting up a new trade, the Income Tax relief is increased from 30% to 50%, but this relief is restricted to an investment of £100,000.

There is no Capital Gains Tax on any capital gains you may receive from an investment in EIS shares or an EIS portfolio. You must hold the shares for at least three years to benefit from this Capital Gains Tax exemption, although it is not withdrawn if you invest the returns in other EIS shares.

Even though there is no Capital Gains Tax on capital gains in an EIS or EIS portfolio, you can still use any capital losses to reduce your Capital Gains Tax liability on other investments or your Income Tax liability if you have no taxable capital gains. Any Income Tax relief you may have obtained on the investment in the shares is deducted before you can then obtain this loss relief.

With an EIS portfolio, losses such as this are worked out independently on each individual share within the portfolio. You may therefore make a gain overall in the EIS portfolio (which is not taxable), but still claim loss relief on losses you have incurred in some individual shares within the portfolio. You also only lose the Income Tax relief on the shares on which the loss relief is claimed; the Income Tax relief on other shares in the portfolio remains.

You can defer any gain you have made in another investment up to three years before and one year after your EIS investment. The amount of gain you can defer is the amount you invest in the EIS; there is no limit on this such as the limit for Income Tax relief. This is only a deferral of the gain, but as long as you still hold the EIS (or a replacement EIS) at the time of your death the gain dies with you.

Combining the Inheritance Tax relief and the unlimited deferral of Capital Gains Tax on other investments can make an EIS a very powerful tool for passing on your estate to beneficiaries without any tax liabilities. As you will see from the example below, it can even mean you are effectively creating an additional tax-free estate for them out of nothing!

### Example 35 - EIS Portfolio

Colin and Melanie Ellis have a substantial net worth. They:

- pay a lot of Income Tax (too much, in their opinion!);
- periodically have Capital Gains Tax to pay on their investments, and;
- know that their estate will have a high Inheritance Tax bill to pay unless they do something about this.

They decide to dip their toes in the waters, and invest £100,000 in an EIS Portfolio.

This investment gives them a £30,000 reduction in their Income Tax. If their Income Tax bill for the current year is less than £30,000 they can get a rebate of Income Tax paid the previous year and pay no Income Tax at all this year.

This means the £100,000 investment has only actually cost them £70,000 after the Income Tax reduction.

They have just sold an investment property for £100,000. They were expecting to pay 28% Capital Gains Tax on the sale, or £28,000. But they can now defer this Capital Gains Tax bill because of their investment in an EIS Portfolio. The Capital Gains Tax can be deferred indefinitely, and it dies when they die, so this is another £28,000 benefit from making the £100,000 EIS Portfolio investment.

After deducting this £28,000 from the net cost of £70,000 this means effectively the £100,000 EIS Portfolio investment has cost them £42,000.

Finally, the £100,000 invested in the EIS Portfolio will not suffer any Inheritance Tax on their deaths, which means they have saved another £40,000.

In total, therefore, Colin and Melanie have a £100,000 investment which they can access at any time they wish but which has effectively only cost their estate £2,000. The summary figures are:

| | | |
|---|---|---|
| EIS Portfolio Investment | £100,000 | |
| *less Income Tax Reducer* | *£30,000* | 30% |
| Net investment after Income Tax | £70,000 | |
| *Less deferred Capital Gains Tax* | *£28,000* | |
| Net investment after Capital Gains Tax | £42,000 | |
| *less Inheritance Tax Reduction* | *£40,000* | 40% |
| Net investment after Inheritance Tax | £2,000 | |

# Chapter 43: Create Your Own Family Investment Company

This is one way you can continue to benefit from most of the growth and/or income from your investments but still put those investments outside your estate for Inheritance Tax purposes.

The amount of growth or income you enjoy is entirely within your control. You simply take whatever you need or want, whenever you want to access it, and leave the rest outside your estate for the eventual benefit of your children.

*Details*

If you create a Family Investment Company you can move some or all your investments into that company. The shares might, for example, be owned as follows:

- Your own shares
- Shares for your spouse
- Shares for your children

Some or all of those shares could be in trust, with specific defined beneficiaries and with you in control as a trustee.

You declare dividends on your own shares, so can retain any income required from the investments, even though the trust or your children owns most of the value of the company. You may also wish your spouse, children or grandchildren to take some of the income, perhaps for Income Tax efficiency, and do so simply by declaring dividends on their classes of shares.

Most of the value of the investment company, and therefore of the underlying investments, will be outside your estate for Inheritance Tax purposes after 7 years even though you can continue to receive benefits from those investments.

# Chapter 44: Have Assets Redirected before You Even Receive Them

If you are expecting to receive an inheritance you can reduce the Inheritance Tax on your own estate by having your parents (or whoever else is leaving this to you) leave it to you in trust rather than passing it on to you directly. This way you can still benefit from the inheritance or gift, but it is outside your estate for Inheritance Tax purposes.

**Example 36 - Redirecting an Inheritance**

Patrick and Veronica Lamb own their own home worth about £500,000 and have around another £600,000 of assets. Here is the calculation of the likely Inheritance Tax bill on their estate:

| | |
|---|---|
| Total Estate | £1,100,000 |

| | |
|---|---|
| Patrick's Nil Rate Band | £325,000 |
| Patrick's Residence Nil Rate Band | £175,000 |
| Nil Rate Band inherited from Veronica | £325,000 |
| Residence Nil Rate Band inherited from Veronica | £175,000 |
| Total Allowances | £1,000,000 |
| | |
| Taxable Estate | £100,000 |
| | |
| Inheritance Tax @ 40% | £40,000 |
| | |
| **Total Estate** | **£1,100,000** |
| Less Inheritance Tax | £40,000 |
| **Net Estate after Tax** | **£1,060,000** |

As you can see, they are therefore expecting an Inheritance Tax bill of £40,000 on their estate before their children can inherit it.

Patrick's parents have both passed away, but Veronica's parents are still alive. Veronica is expecting to receive £500,000 from her parents when they both pass away. Overleaf is what Patrick's and Veronica's estate will be when they receive the inheritance from her parents:

| | |
|---|---|
| Estate before inheritance | £1,100,000 |
| Inheritance from Veronica's parents | £500,000 |
| Total Estate | £1,600,000 |
| | |
| Patrick's Nil Rate Band | £325,000 |
| Patrick's Residence Nil Rate Band | £175,000 |
| Nil Rate Band inherited from Veronica | £325,000 |
| Residence Nil Rate Band inherited from Veronica | £175,000 |
| Total Allowances | £1,000,000 |
| | |
| Taxable Estate | £600,000 |
| | |
| Inheritance Tax @ 40% | £240,000 |
| | |
| **Total Estate** | **£1,600,000** |
| Less Inheritance Tax | £240,000 |
| **Net Estate after Tax** | **£1,360,000** |

If Patrick and Veronica do nothing to protect this anticipated inheritance from Inheritance Tax, the total tax bill on their estate before their children can inherit it will therefore be £240,000 instead of £40,000.

So Veronica encourages her parents to change their Wills, directing the £500,000 into trust instead of passing it directly to her.

Their estate will now look exactly as it did before the inheritance, with a £40,000 Inheritance Tax bill instead of £200,000.

This action alone saves £200,000 Inheritance Tax. On Patrick and Veronica's death their children will receive £1,060,00 directly and £500,000 in trust, which is a total of £1,560,000. They therefore have £200,000 more than the £1,360,000 they would have had if Veronica had not got her parents to divert her inheritance into trust.

As Nelson Rockefeller said, *"the secret to success is to own nothing but control everything"*. Wealthy families have known this and acted on it for centuries. You, too, can do so, starting with your own anticipated inheritance.

# Chapter 45  Turn Your House into an Inheritance Tax Reduction Strategy

For many people their home is a valuable asset which will increase the Inheritance Tax that will have to be paid before their children can eventually receive their inheritance.

It is almost impossible to avoid this tax and continue living in your home.  HM Revenue & Customs get so much tax from houses being passed down the generations that they keep a very close eye on any schemes which attempt to avoid Inheritance Tax on peoples' homes.

One way you can achieve this without causing any problems at all with HM Revenue & Customs is to use an Equity Release scheme and then to invest the cash you receive in an Inheritance Tax reduction strategy.

### *Details*

If you are over 55 and under 85 you can arrange with a specialist mortgage service to "release equity" in your home, turning it into cash.  You remain living in your home, but have converted part or all of its value into cash.

You could, for example, begin "spending your house", i.e. spending the cash you have received in the equity release transaction. Or you could invest some or all of that money in one of the other strategies in this book.

The equity release loan will gradually reduce the value of your estate and therefore the Inheritance Tax payable, although you should bear in mind that the value of your home, which is still in your estate, will probably continue to increase.

Or you could invest the money in an EIS Portfolio as outlined earlier. After two years this is completely free of Inheritance Tax, but you can still draw cash from it if you wish to spend some or all of it.

## Example 37 - Equity Release Strategy

Ian and Rosemary Perkins, both aged 63, are in good health. Their house is worth £1 million, and they have £1 million of other assets, including investment properties, shares and cash.

The current potential Inheritance Tax position is:

| | |
|---|---|
| Total Estate | £2,000,000 |

| | |
|---|---|
| Ian's Nil Rate Band | £325,000 |
| Ian's Residence Nil Rate Band | £175,000 |
| Nil Rate Band inherited from Rosemary | £325,000 |
| Residence Nil Rate Band inherited from Rosemary | £175,000 |
| Total Allowances | £1,000,000 |

| | |
|---|---|
| Taxable Estate | £1,000,000 |
| Inheritance Tax @ 40% | £400,000 |
| **Total Estate** | **£2,000,000** |
| Less Inheritance Tax | £400,000 |
| **Net Estate after Tax** | **£1,600,000** |

They are concerned about the impact on the Inheritance Tax on their estate of any increase in the value of their assets, particularly on the likely loss of Residence Nil Rate Band, which would produce an additional £140,000 Inheritance Tax liability.

Ian and Rosemary release £300,000 equity from their home through a lifetime mortgage.

They opt not to pay any interest, but instead to allow it to roll up, therefore further reducing the Inheritance Tax liability. In their estimate, the increase in the value of their home is effectively frozen, as it is balanced by the increase in the mortgage through the interest rollup.

They then adopt one of the other strategies to place the £300,000 outside the Inheritance Tax loop.

Ian and Rosemary have now obtained the following Inheritance Tax control strategy benefits:

- A saving of £120,000 Inheritance Tax on the £300,000 equity release;
- Reduced risk of loss of the Residence Nil Rate Band, saving another £140,000 Inheritance Tax;
- An effective restriction of the growth in the value of their house for Inheritance Tax purposes.

# Chapter 46: Obtain a Controlling Interest in a Public Company

As already stated, there is relief from Inheritance Tax on their own trading business. But you can also gain 50% Inheritance Tax relief on an investment in a company quoted on the stock exchange, and therefore only pay 20% instead of 40% Inheritance Tax.

*Details*

In order to qualify for Business Relief on fully quoted shares in a public company, and therefore only pay 20% Inheritance Tax, you must obtain a "controlling interest". This means you need to own more than 50% of the voting shares of the company.

You still obtain this Inheritance Tax relief even though you own the shares and can benefit from the capital and any income from those shares.

## Chapter 47: Spend More

Money you spend is not subject to Inheritance Tax.

The more you spend enjoying the good life, the less Inheritance Tax your family will pay. You cannot take your money with you when you die, so enjoy it while you can.

*Details*

If you spend your money and your estate is smaller as a result, the Inheritance Tax on that estate will, of course, be lower.

If you spend it on valuable assets, such as paintings, jewellery, classic cars etc, this is not "spending" money but investing it. Those assets will be a part of your estate and therefore *will* be subject to Inheritance Tax.

The kind of spending that reduces the Inheritance Tax liability is what you might think of as spending to enjoy yourself. Examples include fine dining, playing golf and tennis, other hobby activities, round the world cruises and family holidays with your children and grandchildren.

# Chapter 48: Emigrate to a Country with <u>Low</u> Inheritance Tax

Emigrate to a country with a "death tax" which is lower than the 40% charged in the UK and the total tax on your estate will be lower.

***Details***

If you move to one of the following 33 countries, which have a death tax rate of 10% or less, your children would pay far less than the 40% Inheritance Tax payable in the UK:

- *Algeria*
- *Aruba*
- *Austria*
- *Brazil*
- *Bulgaria*
- *Cameroon*
- *Colombia*
- *Croatia*

- *Curacao*
- *Dominican Republic*
- *Equatorial Guinea*
- *Guatemala*
- *Guinea*
- *Iceland*
- *Italy*
- *Jamaica*
- *Jersey*
- *Lithuania*
- *Montenegro*
- *Mozambique*
- *North Macedonia*
- *Philippines*
- *Poland*
- *Portugal*
- *Puerto Rico*
- *Senegal*
- *Sint Marteen*
- *Switzerland*
- *Taiwan*
- *Thailand*
- *Turkey*
- *Vietnam*
- *Zimbabwe*

The tax implications of moving to another country are not straightforward. If you are considering emigration as a tax strategy it is absolutely essential you take specialist advice.

# Chapter 49: Emigrate to a <u>High</u> Inheritance Tax Threshold Country

If you move to a country which has a higher threshold than the UK before Inheritance Tax is due, less of your estate will be taxed. This could very well mean that the total Inheritance Tax will be reduced, perhaps by a significant amount.

One such country is the United States of America, which is not normally considered a tax haven.

***Details***

Although it is considered a high tax country and has the same rate of death tax as the UK (40%), **the USA *allows you to pass on $11,580,000 before any death tax applies***. You might, therefore, considerably reduce Inheritance Tax or its equivalent, or avoid it altogether, by emigrating to the USA.

The tax implications of moving to another country are not straightforward. If you are considering emigration as a tax strategy it is absolutely essential you take specialist advice.

# Chapter 50: Emigrate to a <u>No</u> Inheritance Tax Country

You could avoid Inheritance Tax or its equivalent altogether if you move to a country which has no such tax.

***Details***

We have identified 85 tax jurisdictions which either do not have Inheritance Tax or any other form of death tax, or do not apply it to estates passed on to your children:

- *Argentina*
- *Armenia*
- *Australia*
- *Azerbaijan*
- *Bahamas*
- *Bahrain*
- *Barbados*
- *Belarus*
- *Bermuda*

- *Bolivia*
- *Brunei*
- *Cambodia*
- *Canada*
- *Cayman Islands*
- *Chad*
- *China*
- *Congo*
- *Costa Rica*
- *Cyprus*
- *Czech Republic*
- *Egypt*
- *El Salvador*
- *Estonia*
- *Fiji*
- *Georgia*
- *Gibraltar*
- *Greenland*
- *Guernsey*
- *Guyana*
- *Hong Kong*
- *Hungary*
- *India*
- *Indonesia*
- *Isle of Man*
- *Israel*
- *Jordan*
- *Kazakhstan*
- *Kenya*
- *Kosovo*
- *Lao PDR*

- *Latvia*
- *Liechtenstein*
- *Luxembourg*
- *Macau SAR*
- *Macedonia*
- *Madagascar*
- *Malaysia*
- *Maldives*
- *Malta*
- *Mauritania*
- *Mauritius*
- *Mexico*
- *Morocco*
- *Namibia*
- *New Zealand*
- *Norway*
- *Oman*
- *Pakistan*
- *Palestinian Territories*
- *Panama*
- *Papua New Guinea*
- *Qatar*
- *Romania*
- *Russian Federation*
- *Rwanda*
- *Santa Lucia*
- *Saudi Arabia*
- *Serbia*
- *Singapore*
- *Slovakia*
- *Slovenia*

- *Sri Lanka*
- *Swaziland*
- *Sweden*
- *Tajikstan*
- *Timor-Leste*
- *Trinidad and Tobago*
- *Tunisia*
- *Turkmenistan*
- *Uganda*
- *United Arab Emirates*
- *Uruguay*
- *Uzbekistan*
- *Vanuatu*
- *Zambia.*

The tax implications of moving to another country are not straightforward. If you are considering emigration as a tax strategy it is absolutely essential you take specialist advice.

# Chapter 51: Gift Assets and Survive 7 Years

You can gift assets of any value to anyone you wish, eliminating the Inheritance Tax, provided you survive at least 7 years after making the gift.

*Details*

Where you know the person who is receiving the gift will never have a large estate of their own, and will therefore not suffer Inheritance Tax when they die, an absolute gift of this kind is a totally effective Inheritance Tax strategy – provided you continue to live for at least 7 years after the gift.

The downsides to this strategy are:

1. You have to continue to live for at least 7 years following the gift, or it will not achieve the Inheritance Tax saving.
2. You can never again benefit from those assets, directly or indirectly, without suffering penalty tax.
3. You have no control over what happens to those assets – they are now completely under the control of the person who received them.

4. The assets are now fully within the estate of the person who received them, and subject to their own Inheritance Tax burden.

If you make the gift into trust you can avoid downsides 3 and 4. As well as having the advantage of remaining under your control (if you make yourself a trustee), a gift into trust can also have the advantage of being protected from the threats outlined elsewhere, including Inheritance Tax for the beneficiaries of the gift.

## Chapter 52: Exempt Gifts

There are 8 "Exempt Gift" strategies as outlined in the next 8 chapters.

*Details*

The advantage over the gifts in the previous chapter is that you do not have to survive 7 years after the gift. The moment you make the gift it is outside your estate for Inheritance Tax purposes.

You cannot benefit personally in any way from the gift. The rules for exempt gifts specify who should benefit from the gift, and you must follow those rules for the gift to be effective for Inheritance Tax purposes.

The downsides of these Exempt Gift strategies are:
1. You can never again benefit from those assets, directly or indirectly, without suffering penalty tax.
2. You have no control over what happens to those assets – they are now completely under the control of the person who received them.

3. The assets are now fully within the estate of the person who received them, and subject to their own Inheritance Tax burden.

If you make the gift into trust you can avoid downsides 2 and 3. As well as having the advantage of remaining under your control (if you make yourself a trustee), a gift into trust can also have the advantage of being protected from the threats outlined elsewhere, including Inheritance Tax for the beneficiaries of the gift.

# Chapter 53: Gifts up to £3,000 per Annum

You can gift up to £3,000 a year without any Inheritance Tax arising. This can be to one person or to a number of different people.

*Details*

You can carry this exemption forward by a year. If you do not use up the entire £3,000 in one year you can add the unused balance to the following year, making gifts up to £6,000.

# Chapter 54: Gifts for Family Maintenance

You can give away any amount you wish without any Inheritance Tax arising provided you can show the gift is required to provide for a dependent relative.

*Details*

A gift for family maintenance may be to provide for the education and maintenance of your children. It could also be to provide for the care of an elderly relative.

# Chapter 55: Small Gifts

You can give away up to £250 a year to the same person without any Inheritance Tax arising.

***Details***

This is called a "Small Gifts Exemption.

***There is absolutely no limit on the number of people who can benefit*** from the exemption. So although the exemption is for small gifts, the total you give away may not be small at all.

You could therefore give £250 a year to each of your children, each of your grandchildren, and each of your great-grandchildren – or to any other people you wish.

There is also no limit on how many years you can do this.

# Chapter 56: Gifts for Weddings and Civil Ceremonies

Within the limits outlined below you can make gifts to anyone when they get married or enter into civil partnership and those gifts are immediately outside your estate for Inheritance Tax purposes.

*Details*

The amounts you can gift are:

- To each of your children - £5,000
- To each of your grandchildren - £2,500
- To anyone else - £1,000

There is no limit on the number of people who can receive Wedding or Civil Ceremony Exempt Gifts.

There is also nothing in the legislation to stop you making more than one gift to the same person if that person legally marries again. If, for example, your child marries, divorces, and then marries again, you could give that child two Wedding or Civil Ceremony Exempt Gifts.

# Chapter 57: Regular Gifts from Income

If you make regular gifts out of income those gifts are outside your estate for Inheritance Tax the moment you make them.

*Details*

You can give away as much as you like without any Inheritance Tax arising if you meet the following conditions:

- It is a regular gift
- It is out of income not capital, and must not reduce your net income below the level required to support your normal lifestyle

You must show it is intended as a regular gift. For example you may give each of your children an expensive birthday present every year. If it is not as clear as this, it is advisable to have something in writing demonstrating your intention to make a regular gift.

If you only gave a gift once and then died, but the paperwork showed you intended to maintain this strategy, this would still be a regular gift.

There is no specific definition of "regular". It could be annual, or monthly for example.

## Example 38 - Regular Gift from Income

Oliver Nicholls is a single man with an estate, worth £3 million, comprising property, cash and investments.

He has an annual income of £200,000 from salary and his investments. He needs £100,000 for his living costs.

Oliver gives £50,000 a year to his daughter Irene. After giving this away he still has surplus income, so he does not need to take any of it from his investment capital.

This regular gift to Irene saves £20,000 Inheritance Tax each year he continues to give it.

## Example 39 - Failed Gift from Income

Kay Bates is a widow with an estate worth £2 million. Her estate consists of her home, worth £1 million, investment property worth £700,000, and cash and other investments of £300,000.

She has an annual income of £100,000 from her investments. She needs £70,000 for her living costs.

Kay gives £50,000 a year to her son Stephen. She funds some of this gift by encashing investments.

Kay hoped that the £50,000 annual gift would save £20,000 Inheritance Tax each year, but it does not save any Inheritance Tax. As Kay had to encash investments, and as a gift of £50,000 a year clearly did not leave her enough income to cover her normal living costs, this is *not* a regular gift from income.

# Chapter 58: Gifts for National Purposes

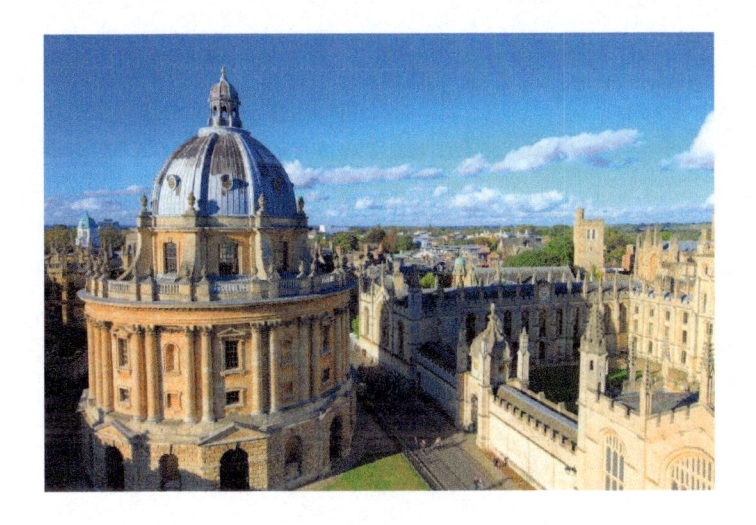

You can make gifts of an unlimited amount to any UK university, the National Trust, the National Gallery, or any other organisation specified by HM Revenue and Customs, without any Inheritance Tax arising.

## Chapter 59: Gifts to Political Parties

If you particularly want a political party to benefit you can make gifts of an unlimited amount without any Inheritance Tax arising.

***Details***

There is nothing to stop you setting up your own political party and funding that with a large donation out of your estate. That donation will immediately be outside your estate.

It must, of course, be a genuine political party rather than simply a way of reducing your Inheritance Tax, and the party must follow all the appropriate rules.

# Chapter 60: Gifts to Charities

You can make gifts of an unlimited amount to a charity without any Inheritance Tax arising. This applies both to lifetime gifts and to gifts made on death through your Will.

***Details***

Whether a gift to charity is made during your lifetime or in your Will it is exempt from Inheritance Tax.

As well as attracting a 40% reduction in Inheritance Tax on the value of the gift, a to charity in your Will can also reduce the Inheritance Tax on the rest of your estate by 10%.

In order to benefit from this additional reduction in Inheritance Tax, the gift to charity must be at least 10% of your total estate less the Nil Rate Band. The remainder of your taxable estate is then taxed at 36% rather than 40%.

## Example 40 - Gift to Charity

Iris Kershaw is a widower with one son, Donald. Her husband, Vincent, passed away three years ago, leaving everything to her.

Iris now has an estate of £5,650,000. She cannot benefit from the Residence Nil Rate Band as her estate is too large for this, but benefits from her own Nil Rate Band and the Nil Rate Band which Vincent did not use.

If Iris left everything to Donald, he would receive £3,650,000 as shown below:

| | |
|---|---|
| Total Estate | £5,650,000 |
| | |
| Iris's Nil Rate Band | £325,000 |
| Nil Rate Band inherited from Vincent | £325,000 |
| Total Allowances | £650,000 |
| | |
| Taxable Estate | £5,000,000 |
| | |
| Inheritance Tax @ 40% | £2,000,000 |
| | |
| **Total Estate** | **£5,650,000** |
| Less Inheritance Tax | £2,000,000 |
| **Net Estate to Donald after Tax** | **£3,650,000** |

Iris, though, is a keen supporter of a local charity, The Donkey Sanctuary. She wants The Donkey Sanctuary to benefit from a £500,000 gift on her death.

The Inheritance Tax calculations taking account of this £500,000 gift are:

| | | |
|---|---|---|
| Total Estate | £5,650,000 | |
| | | |
| Iris's Nil Rate Band | | £325,000 |
| Nil Rate Band inherited from Vincent | | £325,000 |
| Total Allowances | | £650,000 |
| | | |
| Taxable Estate before Charitable Gift | £5,000,000 | |
| Gift to Donkey Sanctuary | £500,000 | |
| Taxable Estate after Charitable Gift | £4,500,000 | |
| | | |
| Inheritance Tax @ 36% | £1,620,000 | |
| | | |
| **Total Estate after Charitable Gift** | **£5,150,000** | |
| Less Inheritance Tax | £1,620,000 | |
| **Net Estate to Donald after Tax** | **£3,530,000** | |

Donald has now received £3,530,000, which is £120,000 less than he would have received if Iris had not given £500,000 to the Donkey Sanctuary. The gap of £380,000 (£500,000 less £120,000) is all from a reduction in Inheritance Tax.

## Chapter 61: Pensions

Your beneficiaries can receive the full amount of your pension investment without paying Inheritance Tax.

However, if you are 75 or older when you die, your beneficiaries can still receive the full amount of your pension investment without paying Inheritance Tax, but will pay Income Tax at their marginal rate on any money they draw from the pension.

*Details*

When you invest in a pension, subject to certain limits, HM Revenue and Customs tops up what you have invested by 25%, immediately increasing the value of the investment, and you can also claim Income Tax relief on 25% of your investment. It is this tax enhanced value which can then be received by your beneficiaries free of Inheritance Tax.

For example, if you invest £80,000 in a pension, the taxman will add £20,000, which means your £80,000 investment immediately turns into £100,000. If you are a 40% taxpayer you then get Income Tax relief, so the £100,000 now in your pension will only have cost you £60,000. If you then die before age 75 your beneficiaries will receive that £100,000 completely free of tax. If you die after age 75 they will receive the £100,000 free of Inheritance Tax but will pay Income Tax at their marginal rate on anything they draw from the pension.

## Chapter 62: Die in Public Service

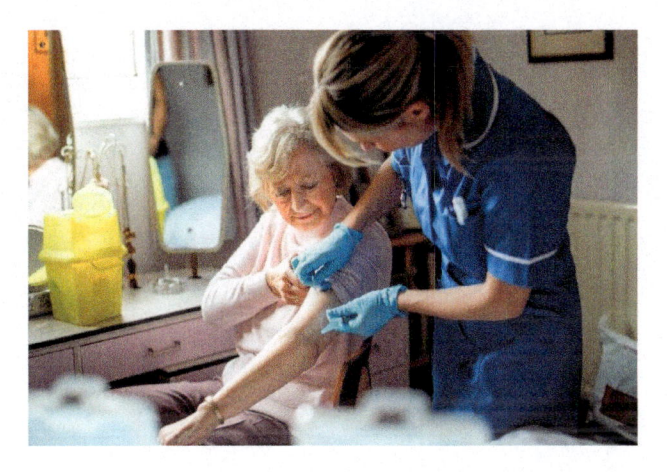

If you are in any of the following positions, whether full time, part time, or voluntary, and you die while on active service, none of your estate will be subject to Inheritance Tax:

a. Armed Forced
b. Emergency Services
c. Humanitarian Aid Work

This exemption also applies if you suffer an injury or disease while on active service and later die from it. It can therefore apply if you are an NHS worker, contract Covid-19 as a result of your work, and die from the illness or complications arising from it.

## Chapter 63: The Next Steps ...

Now you hopefully have a better understanding of the way Inheritance Tax works, whether or not you are likely to pay much Inheritance Tax if you take no action, and some of the actions you could take to reduce or even eliminate your own Inheritance Tax.

We hope you have found this *"Simple Guide to Inheritance Tax"* useful and informative. If you wish to take some advice on the steps *you* should now take to reduce the Inheritance Tax your family are likely to pay, we would be delighted if contacted us for a free initial consultation.

Whether you consult us or another firm that has the appropriate level of expertise, it is absolutely essential that you do use the services of someone who has the specialist knowledge required.

If you had appendicitis, you would not dream of trying to take out your own appendix. You would not even be comfortable with the idea of letting your GP try to operate on you. Clearly this is a job for a surgeon who has been trained how to take out an appendix and how to deal with the many different complications that can arise when doing so.

Equally, planning to control your Inheritance Tax properly can never under any circumstances be a "do-it-yourself" task.

Nor should you expect a general practice

- accountant,
- Independent Financial Adviser or
- solicitor

to be able to handle it properly for you.

Make sure whoever helps you put the right strategies in place knows exactly what they are doing, and understands how to recognise and deal with the myriad of complications that can arise because of your own particular circumstances.

Contact me for further information:

- by Freephone on **0800 488 0907**
- by E-mail at **paul@willstruststax.co.uk**
- or at this address:

>Paul Cadde
>The Oaks
>Lordswood
>Highbridge
>Hampshire
>SO50 6HR

# Appendix

# Trusts

## When and Why did Trusts Arise?

Trusts have been used for nearly 1,000 years to protect family wealth.

They were first used by the crusaders. While they were on their crusade, they wanted to ensure their castle and the rest of their assets were safe and looked after properly. They left their estate in the hands of someone they could *trust* absolutely – a *trustee*. So, their estate was in trust.

## Use of Trusts by Wealthy Families

Once the principle of "trust law" was established, wealthy families began using trusts similar to those originally used by the crusaders. They used them to ensure their castles and other wealth could be passed intact from one generation to the next.

The wealthiest families in this country have always recognised that there are many threats which could attack their wealth. They keep most of their wealth in trust to protect it from those threats.

When their wealth is in trust nobody can insist the family use this for any purpose with which they disagree.

When writing trusts for our clients we usually ensure that key members of the family are trustees, typically alongside professional trustees. We advise our clients to do it this way because professional trustees know exactly how to advise the family trustees and beneficiaries how best to protect the wealth they have in the trust. This means the wealth remains within the control of the "right" family members, i.e. those chosen by the person who originally set up the trust.

### Example 41 - Securing Assets in Trust

Jane King has a house worth £450,000 and £50,000 of savings and investments. She wants to leave all her assets to her son Michael. Her son is facing financial difficulties, is being chased by creditors and may even have to file for bankruptcy.

Jane leaves all her assets in trust for Michael and his children. When she passes away, Michael and his children enjoy the benefit of his mother's assets. They move into the house she left in trust for him. Michael's creditors cannot touch any of the estate passed into trust for his benefit, and even if he goes bankrupt, he and his children can continue to live in his deceased mother's house. All Jane's estate is fully protected for the benefit of her son Michael and her grandchildren, regardless of Michael's own financial circumstances.

### Trusts Protect your Wealth from Threats

It is not just assets of the very wealthy that are under attack. We all face a number of threats to our family wealth, no matter how big or small it may be.

These are the seven main threats to your family wealth:

**Local Authorities** seeking a contribution towards care fees if a family member needs care.

**HM Revenue & Customs** seeking Inheritance Tax each time your family wealth passes down a generation.

**Bankruptcy** of your children. For example if unexpected and uncontrollable changes of circumstance arise.

**Future creditors** of your children. For example if they start a business which then fails.

**Future spouses** of your children. For example if they go through a divorce.

**Future spouses of the surviving partner** after his or her own death.

**Children who become financially irresponsible**. This may be due to circumstances beyond their control, but that does not mean the family should then simply accept the erosion of their wealth. Examples may include falling into bad company, abuse of alcohol, recreational drugs, etc.

## Trusts are for Everyone

We all face the same threats to our wealth.

We can all benefit in the same way from the trust law that was originally intended to protect the wealth of the crusading knights.

The principles of trusts are the same, regardless of the amount of wealth they are protecting.

When you put your assets in trust nobody can make you use them for their own purposes, e.g. care fees, creditors etc.

The trustees must use those assets for the benefit of the people you have said you wish to benefit. These people are the *beneficiaries* of the trust. When writing trusts for our clients we usually ensure that key members of the family are trustees, alongside a professional trustee who is *not* a beneficiary. The beneficiaries may be your spouse, children and grandchildren, other family members, other individuals you wish to benefit from your wealth, or even yourself, and any combination of these.

Your assets are protected from the threats, but still there to be used exactly how you want them used.

You control how the wealth in your trust is used, but that wealth cannot be attacked and does not add to anyone's estate for Inheritance Tax purposes.

*First edition*  *September 2022*

*Second edition*  *December 2022*

*Third edition*  *January 2023*

© Paul Cadde & Graham Dragon

All rights reserved. No portion of this book may be reproduced in any form, (including photocopying or storing it in any medium by electronic means and whether or not transiently or incidentally to some other use of this publication) without written permission from the authors, except in accordance with the provisions of the Copyright, Designs and Patents Act 1988 or under the terms of a licence issued by the Copyright Licensing Agency.

Paul Cadde and Graham Dragon assert their rights as set out in ss77 and 78 of the Copyright, Designs and Patents Act 1988 to be identified as the authors of this work wherever it is published and whenever any adaptation of this work is published or produced, including any sound recordings or films made of or based upon this work.

All of the names and case histories used as examples in this book are fictional. Any similarity with real people or real case histories is purely coincidental.

In the preparation of this guide, every effort has been made to offer current, correct and clearly expressed information. However, the information in the text is intended to afford general guidelines only. This publication should not be regarded as offering a complete explanation of the matters referred to and is subject to changes in law and practice. No responsibility for any loss occasioned to any person acting or refraining from action as a result of any material included in or omitted from this publication can be accepted by the authors or publishers. This work does not render legal, accounting or tax advice. Readers should always consult with appropriately experienced advisers before making or refraining from making any decisions.

## About the Authors

**Paul Cadde**

Paul is the Founder and Senior Partner of *Wills Trusts Tax Solutions LLP*.

He specialises in advising homeowners with children. He drafts Wills & Family Trusts to protect their home and other assets so that their children cannot lose their inheritance due to 12 major threats.

**Graham Dragon**

Graham is a technical specialist at *Wills Trusts Tax Solutions LLP*. He has been a member of Mensa (the high IQ society) for over 30 years. He enjoys spending a large part of his day working on intellectual challenges for the benefit of his clients.

Graham qualified as a taxation technician in 2004. He became a Fellow of his professional association in 2013.

Wills Trusts Tax Solutions LLP

The Oaks, Lordswood, Highbridge,

Hampshire, SO50 6HR

0800 488 0907 (Freephone)

paul@willstruststax.co.uk

www.willstruststax.co.uk

Printed in Great Britain
by Amazon